A NEW MAP OF THE WORLD

A NEW MAP OF THE WORLD

Ian Linden

DARTON · LONGMAN + TODD

First published in 2003 by
Darton, Longman and Todd Ltd
1 Spencer Court
140–142 Wandsworth High Street
London SW18 4JJ

ISBN 0 232 52442 4

A catalogue record for this book is available from the British Library.

Designed by Sandie Boccacci
Phototypeset in 9.5/12.75pt Palatino
by Intype Libra Ltd
Printed and bound in Great Britain by
The Cromwell Press, Trowbridge, Wiltshire

CONTENTS

ACKNOWLEDGEMENTS

I wrote this book in a degree of elected isolation at the bottom of a garden in Suffolk. The nearest sign of globalisation was a migrant Polish agricultural labourer on a tractor in a neighbouring field. The nearest source of books was the Public Library in Halesworth. So my debt of gratitude is that much greater to the many whose insights I have absorbed and stored up over the past years and which appear here, and whom I cannot possibly all name, and the few whose impact was immediate and inspiring during the past two years, whom I can.

Firstly my wife, Jane, who read and pruned my drafts, and contributed her ideas to them. I have also been more than fortunate in having seven other principal readers whose wise criticisms and suggestions resulted, at least in my opinion, in major improvements to the text: Geoff Chapman, Edward Horesh, Timothy Radcliffe, Joan Sharples, Mike Simpson, Denys Turner and my commissioning editor, Brendan Walsh. I am deeply grateful for their time, unstinting kindness and their professional advice of different kinds.

Thank you too to the librarians who got me the books, Jane Davies, Jane Perry and Franscesca Armour-Chelu, for their patience and help, and to Deryke Belshaw, Sophie Linden, Allesandra Masci, Damian Platt, Pamela Murphy, Fiona Scriberras and Toby Wolfe who took trouble to send me key pieces of literature.

Finally I should like to dedicate this book to my ten grandchildren who will need a map and will find out, one day, if this one makes any sense.

IAN LINDEN
July 2003

INTRODUCTION

On the basis of his experience with focus groups a senior policy adviser to a British Prime Minister once complained that electors 'were only interested in shopping and videos'. A partial judgement on human nature from the political elite, you might claim, or hope. He left out sport.

A less partial truth is that people live both in the city of God and in the earthly city, can be rational as well as daft, graced as well as sinful. And an impartial truth is that we must interpret and respond intelligently to the emergent threats and opportunities of a new world if we are to survive. For the twenty-first century is on a trajectory that will threaten the security, freedom and human rights of all of us, not just the poor, yet offers an unprecedented opportunity to tackle the root causes of poverty, wars, terrorist attacks and organised crime, asylum seekers and economic migrants, and the scandalous injustice of inequality.

This is a book about politics on a global scale. My focus group in a development agency, the Catholic Institute for International Relations (CIIR), has for the past twenty years consisted of marginalized people from the 'Third World', and those who worked with them and sometimes spoke for them.[1] They were not saints, nor averse to shopping; several qualified by their courage for torture and imprisonment. My first – and major – premise is a matter of faith, their faith that 'politics' is the hopeful quest for human well-being and flourishing through just forms of governance and social organisation. In other words politics is an ethical quest, to be precise, for justice.

Much of what follows analyses the obstacles to this quest and they are not simply the products of human nature. There are structures of injustice with a life of their own, a global apartheid of rich and poor sustained by those with power to shape global institutions.[2] No sober appraisal of the historical record justifies optimism that a politics of the common good is foreseeable and feasible. It is a matter of 'hoping against hope', speaking truth to power, resisting structural power used against the common good.[3]

So what might be meant by, or assumed to be, the realm of 'politics' forms an unwritten preamble to this book. And different people mean different things by 'politics', more often than not implicitly indicating what are possible and realistic courses for political action to pursue. A self-serving activity of politicians, the state's role in balancing contending interests, the practice of parliamentary democracy and representation of the people, visionary blueprints for society, the art of the possible, and so on, are common enough accounts. Each in turn smuggles in some unacknowledged assumption about human nature and the limits of human agency.

The struggle for justice is thus firstly a struggle for a particular vision of politics. This book, by revisiting the political thought of Thomas Aquinas at the end of chapter two, opts for an account firmly in the classic tradition, politics as an expression of human *moral* agency, however flawed, confused and imperfect. That is why chapter seven looks at the growth of global civil society. Moreover, it has relied on a Thomist view of human nature[4] which, while not optimistic, is hopeful, and while not static, suggests historic continuities. It neither assumes that, as history progresses, most people discover what their real interests are, nor, if they do, that they know how to achieve them – (how could it after the experience of the last century?). But it does assume, *pace* pessimistic Lutheran theology, that they have a capacity to do so and to act accordingly under the right circumstances.

What follows is also based on a number of minor premises. The most speculative of these, explored in chapter five, is that the world we live in is in transition between two epochs: a dying age of industrial production and a new age of the information economy and network society. The coming epoch is necessarily poorly charted, but already intensifying an existing differentiation into areas of affluence and poverty, hinterland and heartland, dominant and subordinate cultures. A patchwork of poor agricultural societies, suffering the depredations of predatory and corrupt governments, war economies and ethnic conflict, largely in Africa, remains trapped in the past, destitute and excluded; the consequences are illustrated in chapter three. The most important characteristic of this contemporary transitional period is an uncontested dominance of a new stage of capitalism in the form of a globalised economy, acting as an interconnected unit in real time and bringing in its wake cultural and social change. How we reached this stage is the topic of chapter four; the variety of resistance to it is discussed in chapter six.

Another – and less speculative – premise is that the political economy of globalisation is best understood as a complex interaction between three forces: the action of states, multinational corporations and the market, predominantly the financial markets. The first two are clearly the product of human agency, susceptible to political influences, the latter, notwithstanding its efficacy in distributing goods, demonstrably a more intractable domain of uncontrolled herd behaviour, greed and fear. Chronic spasms of irrationality grip the market, to some degree, states, and, to a lesser degree, multi-national corporations. The dynamics and direction of the political economy of globalisation thus hinges precariously on the intentions and choices of both individuals and institutions, inside and outside the state. This includes notably inter-state bodies and multinational corporations, each reacting politically to powerful market forces. This theme is also explored in chapter four.[5]

Finally, I would not want to raise false expectations. 'Politics on a global scale' sounds very grand. It is only how we live in the world together – wherein indeed lies an awesome complexity. 'Revisiting Thomas Aquinas' sounds quite impressive too. It means briefly setting out some of the ideas that have shaped Christian political thought as well as getting under this author's skin. For, when it comes to ethics, we have only the resources of the past and the traditions of our different communities. Those are what will be in conversation in any future 'global ethic', not some magical new formula from the alchemists of the lowest common denominator, such as the theologian Hans Kung, with his view that all religions are evolving inexorably towards a few shared principles.[6]

So read this book as a series of snapshots of globalisation – not the ones that are commonly shown in the album of modernity – and as suggestions as to how they might be interpreted. All snapshots tell a story and this is partly my story. They represent a personal attempt to step back from instant advocacy, position papers and baton charges in the streets, to construct a picture out of a contested bundle of facts, to propose a model of ethical enquiry, in other words to make sense of what is going on and what might justly be said and done about it. Living a human life in a future global economy will be no easy matter. There are no apologies if readers reach this conclusion by the end of the book. I have learnt one thing for sure during its writing: it is not in the nature of moral thinking for there to be a single answer that is simple. Yet we must pursue the problematic possibility of finding a moral language for today and tomorrow.[7] For without a shared language we cannot begin to discuss what is to be done.

CHAPTER 1

POLITICAL EDUCATION OF AN NGO-BODY

Large pink expanses denoting the British Empire and tedious films depicting happy smiling natives harvesting cocoa. Geography lessons in a no-nonsense grammar school in the 1950s. This was how many of my generation absorbed their first map of the world.

But as I sat stuffing sweet papers down the old inkwell in my desk, the pink expanses were fast shrinking. Educated Africans had long since stopped smiling at the camera. Ghana's Kwame Nkrumah expressed their aspirations by 'seeking first the political kingdom'. India and Pakistan had already been born in a bloodbath. Now nationalism was spreading like a bush fire in Africa, fanned by Macmillan's winds of change. It should have been the beginning of my political education. And I was blissfully ignorant of it all.

Today, after rearing a family in Africa and working for twenty years in an international development agency with offices around the world, I *feel* less ignorant. Or perhaps just more aware of how reality is distorted and hidden in the prism of contemporary ideology. And aware of the consequences: the lack of urgency about what must begin immediately if human life is not to be 'solitary, poor, nasty, brutish and short' for many; maps of the world charted by the blindfolded, or by fools and knaves; a blundering pursuit of what is right, without ethical signposts. Saturated by lies and half-truths from the mass media and the state, we are losing our capacity for discernment. We cannot see the clear and present danger before us.

The ideology of modern capitalism is sometimes subtle, and

always confusing, and there is little point in tilting at windmills. We need to sweep away the myths to get at the truth. In retrospect as part of 'the ideological apparatus of the state' school was a let down. Imperialism, either rampant or in its decline, was not a subject on the curriculum. Talk of religion and politics was subject to a decent British reticence and shunned. Against the background of the 1950s Suppression of Communism Acts and anti-communist witch-hunts around the world, wise teachers avoided dangerous political ground.

They, the principalities and powers, need not have worried. Politics and history were my blind spots. For no very good reason I assumed that Caesar's Gallic Wars – through which we gamely fought our way in Latin lessons – was fiction. Nor did the dreaded words 'now open your atlases' provoke a prolonged meditation on the works and pomps of the British Empire. I assumed the peoples of the pink expanses enjoyed harvesting cocoa beans and were better off for it. The imperial ideal was unreal and distant, benignly linked to Latin grammar, hot cocoa at bedtime, and the young – long to reign over us – Queen's travels.

Once an elderly history master burst into tears in a lesson about the horrors of the First World War. That the ruling class had done something terrible, and that there was more to wars than daring-do, the more perceptive could conclude from the sudden intrusion of unwanted emotion. The lesson communicated a vague sense that we belonged to more than Britain, to Europe perhaps. But that is where our political education ended. No mention of exactly how the European nations had scrambled for Africa, Britain in the vanguard, of the horrific massacre of Namibians and Congolese, or how disease killed Afrikaner women and children in our concentration camps. How often did I cheer at Saturday morning pictures as our side slaughtered 'Red Indians' or 'Fuzzy-Wuzzies'? Then what could you expect with Richard Hannay, Biggles, Captain Hornblower and Conan Doyle's 'White Company' for heroes? Improving Christmas reading supplied by conscientious parents.

In short there was nothing in my secondary education to induce a 'prise de conscience' or political guilt. None of those 1960s Tory demons were indoctrinating us innocents. Nor was the old, comforting, pink, send-her-victorious map of the world abruptly torn up during adolescence. It just faded away. I was boarding the capitalist roller coaster. 'All fixed, fast-frozen relations, with their train of ancient and venerable prejudices and opinions are swept away, and new formed ones become antiquated before they can ossify', intoned the Communist Manifesto. 'All that is solid melts into air, all that is holy is profaned.' But nobody warned me at Southend High School for Boys.

Ignorance of the world that we were losing, of course, was no recipe for political innocence. We were quietly, subtly and effectively influenced and shaped. The cultural clues for becoming a proper Englishman were uncomplicated but to hand. No need for a wartime Ministry of Information to frame the experience of my generation, to induce us to believe that Britain's past 'civilising mission' was a good thing – unless, of course, unlike me, you happened to grow up in a socialist family. The ideological apparatus of capitalism lay gift-wrapped under the Christmas tree. Pathe Pictorial News did the rest.

For our aspiring, two children, one dog, middle-class family who read the *Daily Telegraph* this view of the world did not appear as subtle political ideology, but simply common sense. The flag was coming down but Britain was doing the decent thing. All that magnificent past with its Fuzzy-Wuzzies, cocoa and Coronations, was being smoothly repackaged as the Commonwealth.

That I belonged to a small warrior nation beset by hubris and fast running out of puff – illustrated so well by Cyprus and the half-baked 1956 Suez adventure – was nearer the truth. Sunday school, Anglican ladies cycling to church, warm beer and cricket on the village green, Ealing comedies, were all so much camouflage. Indeed much of this had been artfully constructed as our national characteristics in wartime propaganda against the Nazis. The truth was that we excelled at war, making money and grumbling. We English had the Maxim gun, the atomic bomb, home-made marmalade and the City of London. And they had not.

We still knew how to conduct counter-insurgency in Malaya and – give or take a few human rights violations – stay on top of the Mau-Mau in Kenya. But after the fall of Singapore, colonial troops between 1940 and 1945 gained widespread experience of the blunders and incompetence of their 'colonial masters'. The game of invincibility was up. Our US allies, like the educated colonial elites, disapproved of colonialism, disliked our 'civilising' pretensions, and were increasingly troublesome. Britain had fought the good fight, but was skint and tired. No more 'imperial preference' or sterling area to shore up the economy but the rigours of the International Monetary Fund (IMF). The pink patches of Empire were soon no more.

The imperial myth was really not much of a cognitive map by the 1950s. A population exhausted by the Second World War was forced into dependence on the USA by 'Lend-Lease' and the Marshall Plan. Eroded by Attlee's necessary compromises, socialist ideals leached out of post-war 'never again' idealism. Empire seemed implausible, incoherent. The deal struck by the USA with a reluctant Maynard Keynes was 'we bankroll you, you give up the Empire'.[1] With the prospect of modest prosperity on the horizon for a rationed Britain, who cared any more about the flag coming down?

Harry Truman laid it on the line in 1947: 'at the present moment in world history nearly every nation must choose between alternative ways of life'.[2] The Korean war, three years later, showed what this would mean in practice. Enter, slowly but surely, the second great map of the world produced in the short twentieth century. A world delineated by the 'Cold War', with an atomic mushroom cloud as its Manichean apotheosis, was not so comforting as the old, but far more compelling.

Like many other people I only understood the Cold War as something real and personally threatening on the eve of the Second Vatican Council, in 1962. As Soviet boats carrying missiles sailed on a collision course with American vessels blockading Cuba, the war suddenly became critically hot. The fear that this might be my last night on earth, or indeed London's last night on earth, followed from the uncertainties of a young Catholic US President squaring up to a Soviet Communist chairman with nuclear weapons. Contemplation of the symmetry of mutually assured destruction as the most cunning of stratagems to preserve the peace had to await the 'wisdom of hindsight'.

Of course, the Cold War was to be lethally hot for millions of people who had the misfortune to live in the midst of the proxy-wars fought between the USA and the Soviet Union, or China, from 1941 to 1991. The starting date of 1941 may sound too early but the violent conflicts between Christians, communists and socialists within European anti-Nazi resistance movements, were implicitly, and sometimes openly, the first proxy skirmishes of the superpowers. The Cold War was like an invasive virus taking hold of societies' DNA. It infected civil wars, ethnic conflict, de-colonisation, struggles for social justice, apartheid and liberation theology, telling bright shining lies about all of them.[3] Often, as a result, the lies came true. The polarities of superpower rivalry infected the framework of political life in the poorest of nations as a self-fulfilling prophecy as 'communist' movements reacted to American-supported oligarchies.

So the map of the Cold War provided an emotive cognitive framework for those developing their first political thoughts in late teens. It was impossible not to situate yourself politically in relation to it. The Berlin Wall provided a powerful symbol manipulated to the full. The 'Iron Curtain' had its geo-political foundations dug at Yalta when Churchill, Stalin and Roosevelt divided up the world into spheres of influence – the story was – on the back of an envelope. The promotion of the 'Cold War' as a frame of reference for thinking about the world was the product of what Eisenhower aptly called the military-industrial complex, a symbiotic power relationship between the directors of military-linked production and top generals and politicians. The needs of military-linked production strongly influenced the economies of the two superpowers, the competing ideologies of the Cold War and the different structures of their core power networks.

Today we know just how asymmetric that 'war' was: the now available footage of Soviet missile sites shows equipment looking like something out of Jules Verne. The Soviet Union was not far off the proverbial 'Angola with missiles'. The bulk of the Soviet military machine was ready for the scrap yard. This at a time when we were led to believe that only our wise leaders could save us from becoming its victims. The gravity of the Soviet threat was a core strand of western ideology. We were made the victims of an odd collusion between the KGB and the CIA, a mutually assured falsehood. As Norman Mailer in *Harlot's Ghost* hints,[4] we had been living through a mutuality of madness.

Europe was harnessed to this superpower rivalry through NATO and a debt of gratitude to the USA. Beyond lay what became known as the Third World, the 'open space or frontier' over which the first two worlds would compete, well beyond the core theatre of the Cold War. The numbering reflected relative economic and military power though not, of course, population size or geographical extent. The Soviet Union formed the second world with China part of the third, hence the later cumbersome phrase 'two-thirds world' denoting . . . not us.

For fifty years the Cold War imposed an increasingly rigid geopolitical grid on a world in which political neutrality was punished. Third World politicians were obliged to adopt the rhetoric of one or other of the superpowers if they wished to benefit from international support. Christians working for social justice or trades unionists fighting for workers' rights risked being branded as communists, and qualified for jail, torture or death. After joining the Catholic Institute for International Relations (CIIR) in 1980, I had the enormous privilege of meeting many of them at critical moments in their lives when they were most under pressure, and of learning from their experiences.

The USA propped up or imposed corrupt and vicious oligarchies and dictatorships throughout the world, though particularly in Latin America. It colluded in systematic torture in Chile, El Salvador and Iran. Communists in Indonesia were slaughtered en masse by the Suharto regime with US blessing. In Nicaragua the United States supported the overt terrorism of the US-armed Contra forces as a result of a near pathological obsession with its Sandinista government. I remember the courage and serenity of one young Nicaraguan agricultural extension worker waiting for her 'turn' in a little rural office after twenty of her colleagues, one after the other, had been assassinated by the Contra.

The Soviet Union, China and Cuba promoted 'Marxist revolutions' in eligible Third World societies with disastrous consequences. An inflated local rhetoric overlaid by a pretentious Marxist jargon justified armed struggle. More often than not it boiled down to the politics of the belly. Impunity from prosecution for the victorious ruling political elite in matters of corruption was the reward of future offices of state. It was not only Che Guevara who was taken in and chased shadows of international revolution through the African bush; so, from the opposing perspective, did the forces of the Rhodesian Front and the apartheid regime. Meanwhile liberation movements that tried to stick to their principles, such as the non-racialist African National Congress of South Africa (ANC), had nowhere to go for the military support that they needed except to the

Communist Parties of the Soviet Union and East Germany. Amongst the democracies, neutral Sweden alone gave the ANC tangible financial backing and, for five years, I felt some of these tensions while acting as the funding liaison between the Catholic Church in South Africa and the Swedish government. The alternative chosen by the Polisario, Eritreans and East Timorese was to struggle on virtually alone, relying on uncertain supplies of weapons, against overwhelming military force.

The Soviet Union and Eastern bloc were a perversion of politics and human society. The death toll of the gulags and Stalinist tyranny were even worse than that of the Nazis. By the 1980s, only isolated pockets of true believers survived within organisations such as the South African Communist party. North Korea was becoming a dangerously isolated political dinosaur with an impoverished, later starving, population. But the products of US intervention in Third World societies – tyrannies and blanket bombing most notably – made the USA an unattractive alternative global political force. Vast tracts of land with their peoples, like Angola and Vietnam, were reduced to total destitution. Cambodia and Afghanistan were devastated. Enduring poverty was ensured. Monstrous fundamentalist regimes swept to power. The hot proxy wars were dirty and merciless. International relations were governed by cynical *realpolitik*.

The Vietnam War seemed at the time the epicentre of this unfolding tragedy. It politicised many in my generation as the Spanish Civil War had in the last. It certainly politicised me, a recent Catholic convert and immigrant in the USA, excited by ideas of social action on behalf of the poor and oppressed. I put pen to paper in protest and, to my amazement, thanks to a doughty Dominican in Dublin, Austin Flannery, had my first article published in 1966 – entitled 'Vietnam and the Christian Conscience'. A position along the lines of 'a plague on both your houses' – and this does not necessarily imply moral equivalence – seemed to me the only moral option. But it left nowhere to go politically – except for a vague form of Third-worldism, *tiersmondisme*, into which I wandered.

It was the peoples of the Third World who were most in need of support, I concluded, and whose suffering was even greater than those who lived under the 'reformed' communism of Khruschev, or suffered Mao's crazed economic experiments. Well, that was as far as I had got when the FBI photographed me in a New York peace march, a child on my shoulders carrying a Vietcong flag. My position as an immigrant, selective Catholic war resister put me punitively high up the Draft-classification list, and FBI photos did not go down well with my employer. I had seen the family from the Dominican Republic upstairs send their sons to Da Nang – or rather heard as the noise above at night abated – and I had no wish to be on the next plane. A hasty temporary retreat from the land of the free to Africa followed.

The interstices of the Cold War seemed the only haven for the political neophyte but they offered only the narrowest of political spaces and some unpalatable choices. It was in the interstices of the Cold War that the struggle for human rights and social justice was mainly going on. Working for human rights resulted in a variety of brickbats – or bullets – according to where you lived in the world. A bipolar world placed anyone active politically within the – today strangely antiquated – spectrum of Left to Right. Third-worldism made of you a good/promotable communist in the Soviet Union and put you squarely on the Left/dangerous side of the spectrum in the UK. Living in this narrow space was to be home for me and for CIIR for many years.

In Africa I learnt about fortitude, bureaucracy, ethnicity, Islam, military coups, missionaries, how to get deported, how French colonialism improved the cooking of fish, and to avoid teenagers with AK-47s, and mosquito nets with holes in them. Meanwhile the 1970s proceeded largely indifferent to this vital store of acquired knowledge. The UK lurched into Bloody Sunday and, under a variety of pressures, not least the IRA, and in a very British covert way towards an embryonic national security state. CIIR earned its first brush with British Intelligence by the middle of the decade, a warning to back off from using a state visit from President Caetano to Britain to highlight the fascist regime's human rights abuses in the Portuguese colonies. This spurred all concerned to increase their efforts.

The centrifugal forces of a bipolar world gradually pushed Third-worldism into more radical directions and the process intensified during the 'second Cold War' prosecuted by Thatcher/Reagan in the 1980s. The infection had been exported from the superpowers and was now entrenched. A visit to northern Namibia, or across the Allenby Bridge from Jordan into Israel, was a visit to oppression by proxy, the same intimidating military installations, the same look on the faces of Palestinians and Namibians. The logic of the Left became compelling. As military pressure was cranked up, the human rights centre barely held. Then the unexpected and unforeseen happened: the Cold War ended.

The combination of an unwinnable arms race, a US-sponsored jihad in Afghanistan, failure to provide the consumer goods of its geo-political rival, and the persistent political fraying of the Eastern bloc satellite states, were too much for the Communist Party of the Soviet Union. The Soviet Union in the Brezhnev era, trapped in a cumber-some command economy, displayed an immobility and inflexibility aptly dubbed 'hibernation'. Most crippling, it was unable to pull itself into the information age. Communism had been a secular religion and the faith had quietly passed away. Mikail Gorbachev, going with the grain of history, presided over the disintegration of his Empire, a cross between a figure from Greek tragedy and a secular reforming pope. Political and economic reform, undertaken together, broke the camel's back.

The crumbling heights of the Russian economy fell like the cheese in Aesop's fable into the jaws of the Russian Mafias, sundry crooks and shadowy *apparatchiki*. A variety of economic carpetbaggers were shooed in by the extremists of American neo-liberalism. National identities – both Lenin and Stalin had retained or given them terri-torial expression, mostly coercively – reasserted themselves, fragmenting the Soviet Union. The rump of Russia increasingly assumed the familiar configuration of a 1970s Latin American oligarchy. Boris Yeltsin was its cunning-clown dictator, embarrassing to his backers, but better than anarchy, ultra-nationalism or a return to the past. Joe Slovo, the intellectual force behind the South African Communist Party, breathtakingly converted it overnight into a pussy-cat social democrat party.[5] Most of the liberation movements quickly went into negotiations. They and the radical Left had nowhere to go but back to the drawing board.

US economic and military power could now be, and was, pro-jected globally without great hindrance, except for China. Francis Fukuyama pronounced the 'universalisation of western liberal democracy as the final form of human government'.[6] A new world order was proclaimed by Bush senior, and in 1991 the US took the opportunity to try out its 'smart' weapons in the first Gulf War.

To define the map of the world that now emerged as imperial in the old imperialist sense is tempting but misleading. Its key characteristics are a quest for predominantly geo-economic power rather than geo-political control, though the latter is deployed to further the former. It involves massive use of military power against a background of 'soft' structural power, shaping culture and institutions in the interests of the USA.[7] The bid by the prominent American academic, Samuel Huntington, to describe the new situation in cultural terms as a 'clash of civilisations'[8] following the shock of the 1979 Iranian revolution, was widely rejected. After 11 September it became too dangerous to restate openly. The clash was transposed into the familiar Manichean idiom of a conflict between Good and Evil. 'The course of this conflict is not known, but its outcome is certain. Freedom and fear, justice and cruelty, have always been at war, and we know that God is not neutral between them,' George W. Bush told Congress having earlier talked about a Crusade.

Summing up the key to this new map of the world by the word 'globalisation' offers a concept whose breadth and variety of meanings encompasses culture while, superficially, avoiding any sense of conflict. The economy and capital play a powerful, quasi-religious role in secular ideology and human relationships. What could be more natural than the elaboration of the myth surrounding them into a new image of the world, *the* global economy? What could better explain the purpose of Liberty's progress through history? The sociologist Max Weber was surely right. 'Not ideas, but material and ideal interests directly govern men's conduct,' he wrote. 'Yet very frequently the "world images" that have been created by "ideas" have, like switchmen, determined the tracks along which action has been pushed by the dynamic of interest.'[9]

The idea of globalisation emerged rapidly as such an organising principle during the late 1980s. It appealed to a wide constituency in the number of new 'tracks' it determined. Attractive to the Right in its emphasis on the global economy and the diminishing role of the state, but also to the Left in giving a new name to the latest stage of capitalism and in providing a rallying cry for campaigning and protest action against the transnational corporations, it was gratefully taken up. Non-specific and multi-vocal, subject to a variety of interpretations, telling a big story about the world we live in, the concept had, as John Gray, Professor of European Thought at the London School of Economics, suggested, something of the character of the last radiance of the Enlightenment before the post-modernists turned off the lights.[10] Corporate business was widely adopting the term as the Berlin Wall was taken apart brick by brick. With it went the second map of the world.

In this new dispensation the directors of Toyota dare proclaim that they are 'bringing the world together' by promoting their stake in the global automobile industry. The French film producer fights to keep Hollywood at bay. The Brazilian peasant finds his family pushed off the land to make way for soya-bean cultivation by agri-businesses. The Japanese banker commits suicide after capital is siphoned out of his bank by speculators abroad, and the young Indian graduate in Bombay and Bangalore succeeds in his country's new information technology industry. All this takes place allegedly as a consequence, or in the name, of 'globalisation'. According to the perspectives of different interlocutors, this is a story about ethics, about communication and interconnectedness, process and policies, culture and justice, progress and underdevelopment.

But pre-eminently it is an account of the growth of a global economy. By this I mean – in the words of the California sociologist Manuel Castells – 'an economy whose core components have the institutional, organisational and technological capacity to work as a unit in real time . . . on a planetary scale'.[11] This is qualitatively different from the internationalised economy of Edwardian imperial Britain. It is a political economy dominated by decisions taken in institutions lying beyond the immediate control of the territorial nation-state, most notably the multinational corporations. It conflates the national and the global as the arena of politics, and creates a dominant network of powerful affluent nodes round the world.

In a remarkably short time 'globalisation' – plus a rehabilitated idea of civil society and Castells' vision of a 'network society' – has filled the vacuum left by the Cold War. It offers a compelling cognitive mapping of the world, the new common sense, an ideology for the twenty-first century. In no less time a range of political positions has grown up in relation to it. These have generated some spectacular street clashes between police and protestors around big international governmental gatherings, in Seattle in 1999, Prague in 2000, and Genoa in 2001. The flow of books and articles on the topic has yet to be staunched. Globalisation has become news. Churches, development agencies and politicians rush to defend, attack, promote, restrain and generally come to grips with it as a process and policy. Each seems sure that it is good, or bad, or both, though it is far from clear that they are all talking about the same thing. It is as if we are in a David Lynch film, mystified by what is going on, but determined to infuse it with our own moral meaning.

Unlike Lynch movies we are not dealing with an abstract reflection on meaning in the cinema of illusion, but how some human beings make a living and how others die as a consequence. Economics, how human beings make a living, is part of culture, the behaviour we are accustomed to, and the choices that we make. However much we persist in dividing up reality into disciplines that are conveniently studied as a unit, the texture of societies is, amongst other things, the texture of the social relationships created as we make our living. Because of the way we structure our society around economic activity and the prevailing ideology that justifies this way of living, economics has become a core problem for ethics.

As if this were not difficult enough, ethics itself has become an acute problem for societies such as ours. In a pluralist society and world we are daily aware that not everyone comes to the same moral conclusion about the same human acts and behaviour. Nor is it immediately clear what the foundations of ethics are in a secular society. How is it possible to evaluate globalisation, to share moral guidance if our moral toolkit got lost somewhere down the line? This loss is sometimes glimpsed as a key difficulty in dealing with new questions arising from technological advances in biology and medicine, but it is no less true of the pressing problems of how we make a living in what we are coming to describe as 'the global economy'. These questions are addressed in the next chapter.

Being part of a particular historical and global community, the Catholic Church, makes available a tradition and moral resources that may profitably be drawn on, and elaborated, and that may be helpful to more than Catholics. Words and ideas such as sin, as in the seven deadly sins, and virtue, as in the cardinal virtues, part of a shared Christian heritage, are unfashionable. But their meaning can be – I would suggest must be – rehabilitated for the future. For though we have moved on massively in the realm of technology and science from the Middle Ages, human progress in the moral sphere has been slow, intermittent and sometimes retrograde. This is a dangerous imbalance. For a generation that despises the past, wants its religion to be 'new age', and its morality to be invented on the hoof in a headlong rush into the future, the beginning of historical humility is the beginning of wisdom.

CHAPTER 2

DIALOGUE
VERSUS FLAT-PACK ETHICS

When you work in a non-governmental organisation (NGO), particularly a development agency, you come across a high concentration of people with strong views about how the world ought to be – and equally strong views about the organisation in which they work, sometimes as a consoling diversion from the intractability of the world. It is called being 'values-led'. Where the values lead you, and what exactly they are, is the problem.

It was some time before I realised that to give an honest and precise account of the values floating around in the ether, and occasionally landing with a splat in trades-union meetings and staff discussions, was no easy matter, like trying to nail down a blancmange. And this was not some special failing of moralistic NGO-bodies, but a pervasive quality of our society and time. What follows tries to explain why this should be, with some tentative suggestions about whence an account of ethics in a time of globalisation might be derived and how it might be applied. For, when it comes to global poverty and the destruction of our environment, few want to sit on the fence, and fewer enjoy the prospect of running around gloriously, but aimlessly, on top of it.

The twentieth century in which this narrative is rooted has been aptly called the century of the Self, a century of 'me, my, and mine'. Yet in the last fifty years, the 'I', the 'acting subject', faced dissolution in two completely different ways: in practice, in the utter helplessness of Hitler's concentration camps; and in theory, an intellectual consequence of the spread of Freud's thought and French post-modernist philosophy. From the impact of psychoanalytic theory to the use of St Ignatius' spiritual exercises in religious retreats, from the influence of Michel Foucault's thought to research into the biochemistry of the brain, the concept of 'the person in community' was subjected to a sustained critique.

At the same time, the communal 'we', our belonging to a group or a community, our social identity, was never more problematic. The Holocaust, Stalin's pogroms and the threat of nuclear war hung over the latter half of the century, terrible symbols of how, through the manipulation of nationality and ideology, the communal could bring about mass annihilation. There was no escape from the threatened 'me' and 'mine' into collectivism.

In defiance of this tortuous path to nihilism came the assertion of human rights, taken up into the framework of international law in the UN Charter and Declaration of Human Rights and its protocols, as the contemporary means of resolving the clash between the collective – notably Nation, Party, Religion – and the individual. The individual had inalienable rights. The state had to protect, nurture and realise them. Human rights, individual rights or entitlements, re-emerged from the shadow of the Second World War to become the way to talk about ethics through law, and the means to say 'never again'.

It seemed a hopeful escape from a dialectic of despair, the last possibility for a common language of politics in a world that showed every sign of having lost the foundations for any shared ethics. Indeed 'modernity' – a construct of modernisation theory that saw human development as the quest to enlarge human freedoms and choice after totalitarianism – defined itself principally as the attribute of those using human rights language. The growing core list of what human beings may fairly expect to enjoy in their lives, their human rights, describes today what growing numbers around the world believe is necessary for their well-being – however variously 'well-being' may be conceived. In short, the realisation of human rights is the necessary condition for human happiness; indeed, it is the dominant contemporary way of talking about how to be happy, about ethics.

Rights language now lies at the heart of a humanist faith and hope in betterment. This may arguably not yet be a universal language –

there are other ways to talk about how to be happy – but it is promoted as such, and has striven to be so since its codification in United Nations protocols. This is the nearest we get to the framework of a shared and popular ethics in a plural world. While there may be dispute about applying the list to everyone in all contexts, most people will accord most of the list to all people.

Consideration of children somehow focuses these moral propositions in popular thought. A Palestinian or Israeli child torn to pieces by explosives brooks no argument. The denial of human rights to children, transgression of the rights of the young and vulnerable, adds a potent emotional dimension to demands for the acceptance of 'rights language'. Indeed, denial of the items agreed by states as properly included on this list, or their transgression, defines how secular thought sniffs around the dangerous religious concept of sin.

HUMAN RIGHTS TALK

It goes without saying that human rights language became an important political weapon in the hands of the First World during the Cold War. Talk about human rights became an aspect of projecting soft power. The USA, for example, often used other states' human rights violations as a propaganda weapon in the struggle for 'the moral high ground'. Like any other high ground, it was worth occupying in order to attack the enemy more effectively.

To describe this process as the 'politicisation' of human rights might give the impression that human rights talk lacks the dimension of a political project. Politics, the way we organise human society, is a fundamental dimension of ethics. Human rights language, in as much as it is a modern way of talking about ethics, is a discourse about human relatedness, about how we are in the world with each other, about the content of politics. Amnesty International, of course, has championed the most political example of human rights talk in the sense of expressing an absolute faith in a checklist of rights as the dominant project for human flourishing and wellbeing – not, it should be underlined, because it has shown a bias for any existing political group or party.

When I first undertook commissioned work for CIIR, the organisation was coming into minor prominence. It had co-published in May 1975 a dramatic booklet *The Man in the Middle* with the Rhodesian Catholic Commission for Justice and Peace. This detailed human rights violations by the Rhodesian Front forces and was in many ways an archetypal document of Catholic modernity. The title referred to the neutral innocence of those caught in the crossfire between two contending political projects, Smith's brutal quest to retain white supremacy through the Rhodesian Front and the Patriotic Front's armed struggle to regain the land and take power. How many 'men' were at the time 'in the middle' was a moot point.

The human rights language of the booklet provided a semi-protected way to enter political debate and advocacy. The title, in the charged atmosphere of the late 1970s, sought to gainsay any specific political project, though the publishers, CIIR, were clearly in favour of one prospect: democracy and thus black-majority rule. A British judge had ruled already against Amnesty International being given charitable status because the overriding nature of its work was the 'promotion' of human rights. CIIR was a registered charity, so some concern for 'protection' from potential detractors was prudent.

The Man in the Middle was intended to discredit the Smith regime and to counter the Smith propaganda machine. It was only later, in a published *Rhodesia to Zimbabwe* series, that CIIR set out what specific changes in a number of sectors, education and agriculture for example, would, in its opinion, be required for well-being and a just society in Zimbabwe. This amounted to a radical, democratic dispensation for the new nation.

I remember at the time chafing at the limitations of the language chosen to talk about change. How was it possible to move logically from a pose of God's eye neutrality, which *The Man in the Middle* sought to achieve, to the difficult political task of talking to different interlocutors about what might become of Zimbabwe – or Namibia or South Africa come to that? And how could there be a place of neutrality between the torturer and the tortured? Despite the good intentions, there seemed something inherently dishonest about it all. I suspected that Christopher Hitchens was right. 'The truth never lies,' he once said, 'but if it did it would lie somewhere in between.'

My crude intuition was that two 'levels' existed amongst activists: a 'human rights level' of commitment, with the possibility of retaining clean hands, and, what seemed to be more fraught with danger, a political level of commitment which meant taking sides, taking risks and proposing futures. The latter, where Pastor Dietrich Bonhoeffer had ended up in Nazi Germany, could clearly be costly. Indeed CIIR later published a short pamphlet by the South African Dominican theologian, Albert Nolan called *Taking Sides*, rejecting neutrality, which sold a remarkable number of copies. But I was not sure how to move honestly from one discourse to the other, or how they related. There was just the insight into the necessity of Christian political commitment with all its dangers, potential betrayals and disappointments.

My deeper initiation into the core concept of human rights proved challenging. Rights turned out not to be things primarily that you 'had' as an individual, like a liver, and that could be abused, but things that were socially recognised and realised, that were exercised by a member of a particular society, as a product of a particular form of human relatedness. They were what were acknowledged as being owed to people, their due, by virtue of their needs or nature.

'Rights' crop up in easily recognisable form in England at the end of the fifteenth century in the communal setting of the Christian parish, used in the context of a parishioner's annual reception of the Blessed Sacrament. 'Taking' or 'receiving your rights' meant receiving Holy Communion from the priest. This depended on the fulfilment of social and religious obligations that defined the holder of these rights as a member of the Body of Christ.[1] In no sense could the communicant 'own' the sacred host nor did he or she have an 'individual' right to communion; rather the Host was what was due by reason of a person's 'social' belonging as defined by Church membership.

But this was only one strand of a natural rights tradition. The idea of *ius*, what is just, began to be used in the Roman law sense of a 'right over or to something', *dominium*, in the canon law of the twelfth and thirteenth centuries, most notably as a right to self-preservation. This was the strand of natural rights that rights language later elaborated in modern secular usage. A right became the antithesis of the communal, an assertion of 'mine against yours', to be precise an absolute claim to power over private property – and over the self in the sense of liberty – rather than any practice of shared use.[2] Locke and Hume were much exercised in justifying this state of affairs. Over four centuries claims of this nature slowly gained ground and proliferated, most often as a consequence of social and political struggles or changes of power between groups and classes, sometimes as a formal Bill of Rights (1689). The entitlements and liberties implied in such imagined, inalienable endowments only made sense as a claim on somebody or some corporate legal entity. As formulated in the UN Charter, this legal entity was, of course, the sovereign member state.

So the question arose what happens to human rights when states cease to exist, as in parts of Africa during the 1990s, or when states obviously are unable to realise a particular entitlement single-handedly, as most notably in the right to development? And what of the diffusion of rights language that allows it to be claimed that animals have rights, that there is a 'right' to abort a Down's syndrome baby in the womb, or, come to that, a right to free health care at the point of delivery with no obligation to pay the taxes that make this possible? As part of what became known – with subtle elitism – as the 'human rights community', working in an organisation using rights language, I found these troubling questions.

Moreover, there was a convenient fit between the subjects of human rights discourse and the sum total of individual wills and choices which liberal ideology saw as the subjects of the 'market'. Human rights projected into human nature as its inalienable attributes were naturally attractive to 'market man'. The setting of human rights firmly in a sphere of personal choice was greatly reinforced by the growth of market society.

The 'meta-ethics' of the market – not 'business ethics' but its Big Idea – has as its only proclaimed value to increase the amount of individual choice. Indeed, considered as a political agent in the neo-liberal Thatcher–Reagan years, the subject of this choice was portrayed by preference as an instance of the autonomous individual 'consumer'. The idea of choice is thus easily reduced to selecting from a range of things to buy and own. And individuality is correspondingly reduced to an attribute derived from distinct patterns of consumption and consumer choices. That just about empties out the ethical content from politics to leave the idea of a political community out in the cold.

Max Weber saw that political community requires 'value systems ordering matters other than the directly economic disposition of goods and services'.[3] Otherwise from where can the concept of citizenship arise? Perhaps the root problem of liberal capitalist society simply is its lack of political community. And this is why our values flap around in the breeze with gaping holes in our ethics. This is certainly the central dilemma of 'Third Way' social-democratic and liberal forms of government. Freedom to choose, tolerance and respect for 'the other' are essentially formal values. Easy to tick the box. But they lack content and substance. They do not indicate what kind of society 'we' would like to be living in ten years hence and why. Nor how it might be organised and got to work. In this sense the values that 'we' might agree on do not represent a coherent political project.[4]

Indeed, the contemporary use of the word 'community' indicates that it functions as a sweetener sprinkled like ketchup on unpalatable levels of fragmentation and human isolation. People no longer 'live in community'. They choose 'lifestyles'. These lifestyles segment the market and direct the growing use of advertising, the secular catechism of choice. In turn advertising reinforces segmentation. Conduct is not right or wrong but 'appropriate' or 'inappropriate', as if it were on a par with a fashion accessory. Lifestyles are more or less fashionable ways of being human. 'The community' really exists either as new – or old – forms of exclusive identities, for example particular and often small ethnic and religious communities, and narrow 'interest groups', or finds expression in some more universal way such as in powerful institutions of the state like the National Health Service with its special values. The relationship between the two modes is that the former makes claims on the latter.

This was the world in which Margaret Thatcher could confidently assert that society did not exist, only individuals and families. But it was no less the political world created by specific policies in which she tellingly denounced the inertia of welfare state Britain created by her predecessors. Those with entitlements sought them from the state. They were dubbed 'scroungers'. She meant, I suppose, after due allowance for the poisonous political rhetoric, that they enacted a diminished citizenship as a result of enforced passivity.

This conjuring up of the image of the social security recipient passively engaging with the state from behind protective glass remains evocative, and in more ways than the Thatcher government intended. It offers a microcosm of the wider liberal society in which, in growing areas of life, citizenship is reduced to the consumption of, and claims on, different classes of 'goods' – understood in both the material and abstract sense. Some of these may be, and are, conceived of as rights.

NGOS AND THE ARBITER STATE

This fundamental relationship of the state to people has inevitably informed popular views of what constitutes legitimate political engagement. As Rowan Williams writes, 'the purpose of political action, on such models, is to persuade the power-holder to honour or realise the rights of the citizen'.[5] The problem with this model is that it transforms the political arena into a terrain of jostling claims and counter-claims made on the state, with the state imagined to be acting impartially between them. The citizen pre-eminently enters the political terrain as bearer of sectional, or sectarian, demands on the arbiter-state.

In this arena of conflicting claims there is no place for any radical challenge to each entitlement claim or proclaimed liberty, no way to adjudicate whether it is a broad social good being sought rather than the good of 'mine against yours'. Those, for example, claiming the 'right' to three single vaccinations, rather than a triple vaccination (MMR), against the childhood diseases, measles, mumps and rubella, provide an instructive example. They do not recognise the social consequences of their claim because they have been morally formed in a discourse of 'my good' (or in this case the emotive 'my baby's good') of avoiding a supposed risk of autism. This overrides any grasp of the simple social good of 'herd immunity' best achieved by MMR against contagious diseases that equally threaten others. Such conflicts over 'rights' ought to provide an opportunity for all concerned, politicians and parents, to debate society's weak understanding of risk and the social good. But, of course, this is precluded by the nature of the conflict, which involves an absolute individual claim against a poorly formulated idea of the common good.

The same dynamic of political engagement applies to NGOs and 'pressure groups'. The problem, of course, is noted by the Right in relation to claims by trades unions, but it applies to all 'interest groups'. It is characteristic of modern political 'dialogue'. It is observable most obviously in 'rights' based conflict about abortion. Here, debate seems deliberately to preclude a challenge to the ethical foundations of each position in favour of the emotive assertion of the starting point of each side's argument: the supremacy of the mother's autonomy and choice, or religiously based assertions about the beginning of human life, its divine origins, and the corresponding rights of the human embryo as a potential person. This conflict is often described as a product of the clash between traditionalism and modernity, in particular between Catholicism and liberalism, but it is far deeper than that.

Now, the normally attributed nature of the 'traditional' – the artificial social construct understood as the contrary of modernity – is that the communal, social and 'traditional' limit the freedom of the individual and circumscribe choice. Few living in an African village would argue with that. It is the dominant theme of many twentieth-century African novels. But Rowan Williams suggests that the politics of modernity and liberalism also constrain genuine open-ended dialogue about individual and social 'goods'.[6] This would be the indirect result of politics in a time of proliferating human-rights-style claims on the state by contending interest groups. To ask radical questions during competitive bargaining and litigation is ruled out. As with the vaccination, abortion and workers-rights cases, the prosecution of claims for rights on the state invariably precludes a political process that enables contending parties to reach a position more than trivially different from their starting point and corresponding to what might be called 'the common good'.

But an alternative political process is possible. 'Ideally this process is one of defining what is arguably good in some measure for all involved; and thus one of discovering in what ways my good is "invested" in yours,' Williams writes.[7] Or put in another way this political process is a shared quest for how human rights discourse and talk of the common good might coalesce to generate a new unified language and a radical politics. Such would be the basis of a genuinely deliberative and transformative Christian politics and ethics that incorporated the significance of the nation-state, while going beyond it.

This is today's ethical quest. In the twenty-first century it can only have hope of success by working in the international or global context of the universal common good. Indeed the liberal ethics of

John Rawls in his *The Theory of Justice*, written in the early 1970s, seems quaintly dated in its failure to think outside the boundary of the nation-state.[8] Nonetheless, the ethical insights that arise from action at a national level can be applied to guiding the embryonic growth of supranational institutions and steering existing international bodies. For the national is increasingly a particular aspect of the global, subject to the same forces and ideologies. Faced not least by ecological crisis, the disparate international political actors of the contemporary world need urgently to seek what is good for themselves, in terms of the correct investment in the good of others.

There is a profound as well as an obvious reason why this does not happen. In the Dominican Herbert McCabe's words 'a certain distortion of the nature of man is built into the capitalist culture which makes it difficult for us to recognise ourselves for what we are, to recognise, in fact, what we want.'[9] The same could, and would, be said by Marx of feudal and tribal societies, and by others of recent communist societies. This could be put in a more robustly Augustinian way by using the language of 'sin' to describe the condition and its consequences. And this is why radical ideas of ordering the way we are in the world together, the politically possible, become merely utopian, and we conduct our ethical thinking behind a screen of alienation and self-deception. How we get to happiness is something about which we are predisposed to be wrong.

So the fly in the ointment is obvious. But unfortunately, the account of how we get things wrong introduces apparently insoluble dilemmas: dichotomies between freedom and obedience, self-interest and the common good. McCabe for one will have none of it. 'Ethics is entirely concerned with doing what you want,' he wrote, 'that is to say with being free. Most of the problems arise from the difficulty of recognising what we want.'[10] So how do we develop an 'eye' for the good?

A prerequisite for getting our ethics right, Rowan Williams suggests, depends on a willingness to risk participating in open-ended dialogue. This may take us politically where we do not want to go, into the consequences of 'seeing the other as involved in exactly the same history of risk, error and unacknowledged need of the other as oneself'.[11] In short, it involves us recognising ourself in the stranger, the economic migrant, the Muslim, the rival claimants on family, national or global wealth, and thus rediscovering the 'I' anew through the 'We'. It therefore means making an imaginative leap into a narrative other than our own personal, religious or national biography. And, subsequently, our willingness to be changed by such a dialogue.

This is when alarm bells ring. The conversation has reached the limits of a secular world view. For amongst the possible outcomes of such a leap – and I would argue the only realistic outcome – is the entry into another and theological narrative, a story about the purpose of creation. 'We can see', Herbert McCabe wrote, 'that ethics is the quest for less and less trivial forms of human relatedness. In this quest ethics points towards, without being able to define or comprehend, an ultimate medium of human communication which is beyond humanity and which we call divinity.'[12] It would be disingenuous to pretend this was not the horizon of Christian politics even if all the attention is necessarily on the journey towards it.

So, in summary, ethics for a time of globalisation cannot be a given, is not a neat set of rules, or even a helpful manual for assembling an acceptable way of living – though such an outcome may result from a usable ethics. Ethical behaviour demands reflection and dialogue on the complex interactions of politics and economics. What is to be done cannot simply be read off human nature, for our ideological distortions are projected into it. 'It is evident', Marx wrote, 'how political economy establishes an alienated form of social intercourse as the true and original form and that which corresponds to human nature.'[13] Demythologisation is no purely academic exercise, but an urgent necessity to avoid being diverted by the dominant ideological account, however subtle, of what it is to be human and as an antidote to the alienated nature of human relatedness. Apparently irresolvable conflicts of an ethical kind may begin to disappear, or, at least may be understood in a more integral way, and the simple demands of justice emerge more clearly.

CONCERNING SECULAR CERTAINTIES

On this analysis NGOs are handicapped in their approach when it comes to undertaking a political or ethical project beyond the diminished account of ethics provided by human rights discourse –

though most try. My experience of advocacy in NGOs over the years, both those based on Christian and secular premises, is that many of them would like to explore ethics more.[14] Yet little radical self-questioning is undertaken in order to discover a usable ethics and situate the programme of each organisation within it. It is not that the answers given by NGOs are necessarily wrong, but that fundamental questions are not asked.

When it comes to an alertness to the problem of ideology and the need for demythologisation, many NGOs rank lower than most of the 'mainline' Churches and their agencies. Perhaps it is because they have been subject to far less criticism and critique. Most, if not all, seem unaware of the problems of mixing common good and human rights languages uncritically, particularly in their advocacy. Most, if not all, are happy to work within a model in which NGOs make claims – sometimes conflicting claims – on states or inter-state bodies, on behalf of – or with – chosen third parties. These third parties, often similar organisations with far less resources based in the 'Third World', are loosely lumped together, and get described, more hopefully than accurately, as 'the poor', or now more often as 'partners'. Moreover, claims are made with the kind of stern moral rectitude of the nineteenth-century Christian missionary.

The insight that the practice of justice, peace and development must entail genuine open-ended dialogue between a large number of interlocutors, including governments and international financial institutions, came late to the scene. The idea was not greeted with universal acclaim at the beginning of the 1990s. The identity of many NGOs dealing with the environment and international development was fragile, more often based on contestation: what they were against, rather than what they proposed. To a great extent in the UK such a dialogue was pushed forward by the incoming New Labour government. And, indeed, outside of a few Christian development agencies, it was considered novel that the Christian tradition may still have something specific to contribute to this dialogue, other than warm bodies in demonstrations and motivated, willing donors. A surprisingly narrow and secular view of the world prevailed in organisations dealing daily with poor people living in religious cultures.

It hardly needs saying that writers such as Rowan Williams and Herbert McCabe have not grown from some intellectual *tabula rasa*.

Their depth of insight is inseparable from their membership of a religious tradition. But these traditions are only superficially acknowledged in much of the NGO world, their truth claims tolerated only according to their immediate utility. It is as if the urgency of the secular quest for goodness, and unity, makes it permissible to override equally important values of truth. 'Winning' the current 'issue' becomes the most important political question.

In consequence, the moral or merely strategic questions posed by globalisation appear pre-wrapped as 'issues' to be won or lost. This has a number of consequences. It leads to the differentiation of disparate new interest groups. This in turn can make the generation of a new, coherent, democratic political project more distant. The reduction of the content of politics to a cluster of 'issues' makes it an easy matter to prescind from the radical ethical, and therefore profoundly political, question: what might be meant by acting for the good nationally and globally? Not an easy question to ask without sounding precious. A reticence in this regard is probably felt, at some level, to be required in a multicultural society. In a world where there are fears that no *a priori* guarantee of fundamental agreement exists on more basic ethical fundamentals, perhaps better to keep quiet. A reluctance is encountered on all sides to go beyond 'issues' into deeper waters. In this way the associations of civil society, the notional space between government and family, have become in some aspects of their work the inadvertent ideological bearers of the post-modern order. The risk is that they may fragment our politics even more. The test is whether they make any broad conversation about our political future more difficult or facilitate it.

So, by default, political discourse led by government defines a decreasing number of options and becomes focussed, beyond upholding a few ill-defined values, on managing the 'delivery' of a limited number of social goods. The top priority of governance then too easily becomes techniques to control the financial workings of the economy and to control the opinion-forming potential of the mass media when there is loss of control over 'delivery'; and the economy is managed primarily to regulate the consumption of goods. This confirms citizens in their identities as 'consumers' rather than citizens. The lowest, most peripheral form of the politics of consumption, defined by the inability even to be a consumer, is the 'politics of the belly', politics for the poor, the management of starvation in several sub-Saharan countries. Politics has become trapped in a self-perpetuating loop.

At the same time the techniques of persuasion, advocacy for certain political options, our reduced, modern form of classical rhetoric, becomes limited to three moods. Firstly comes the most vicious – the evocation of fear. Terrorism, possession of weapons of mass-destruction, narcotics, HIV/AIDS, mass migration of populations, fundamentalism and so on, are marshalled by elites as key reasons for taking a particular course of action or following a particular policy. This tactic worked for the good with the Victorians when the dreadful health of the urban poor was seen as a threat to the middle classes. Contagion is a powerful idea. Reform took place for a variety of reasons, including fear of the spread of disease. Fear will probably work again though not in a desirable way. The fearful society of the USA is swamped by handguns and a majority are easily induced to support wars in contravention of the UN Charter.

The other two moods are less immediately damaging in their impact but, when pitted against each other, are effective in rendering further reflection otiose: these are self-interest and moral concern. Put forward, one after another, as two contending reasons why a policy should be pursued, morality comes in usually as a last-ditch recourse after appeals to self-interest have failed. Thus morality is presented as the antithesis of self-interest, an instrument to be used when all else has been tried on voters, or when the policy elite remains unmoved. At that point, morality becomes the garment put on to cover a fearful nakedness, but, seen like a puritanical hair shirt, is doomed to being unpersuasive. The trick, of course, is never to say what is meant by 'self-interest' – or indeed 'national interest'.

So what happens when we do 'unwrap issues' and consider them ethically in dialogue rather than take them as a fixed claim? The short answer is apparently irresolvable dualisms: communal goods versus my good, common good discourse versus human rights language, private versus public, political versus religious, individual versus society, freedom versus obedience, to mention the most recurrent. As discussed above, human rights suddenly become problematic. Would that we had an ethics fit to investigate the validity of these apparent conflicts. But we are, in such matters, heirs to a historic collapse of moral understanding and moral formation, charted lucidly by Alistair Macintyre in *After Virtue*.[15] That is why the moral confidence of many NGOs and interest groups, walking on water, sometimes seems mildly frightening.

REVISITING THOMAS

It really is a case of 'I wouldn't start from here.' Secular modernity and post-modernism have turned out to be ethical cul-de-sacs. We may have walked into them for the best of reasons. It really does not matter. Any residual consensus on moral values is now coming apart in front of our eyes. In order to advance beyond this impasse, we have to retrace our footsteps. Or to rephrase a metaphor from the Peruvian liberation theologian, Gustavo Gutierrez, we need to draw on some deep wells, covered over by the passage of time.[16] The task is nothing short of re-establishing an ethics and politics that make possible genuine political discourse and dialogue leading to action for justice. And for such action to be effective in a democracy necessarily implies the transformation, or formation, of political parties. Knowing this is the beginning of NGO humility.

It is only as far back as the mid-thirteenth century, and with Thomas Aquinas, that we regain an intellectual terrain that offers some glimpse of how what now seem to be insuperable difficulties might be overcome. And this is another country in all its medieval strangeness. Yet it is only at this remove that our cultured dualisms, our dichotomous key to moral crisis, recede into the deeper problem of what it means to be human – despite all the questions that the medieval synthesis leaves unanswered. It is surely by going back to a basic anthropology that a distinctive and coherent ethical and – therefore – political project becomes possible for today.

But how could anyone suppose that something this far away from our contemporary way of thinking had anything to say to us? That revisiting Aquinas' framework for a unified moral theory at first, and even second glance, seems such an eccentric resort, is part of our problem. It is a measure of our contemporary lack of historical humility. Nonetheless, in our contemporary political impasse it makes sense to recover and re-appropriate lost insights from the past. The past is not the disposable husk of the present, especially if we have this gnawing sense of having mislaid something important, some lost wisdom. And, however difficult, the retrieval of an integrated ethical/political framework is essential for evaluating something as potentially epoch-making as globalisation and clarifying the ethical dilemmas it contains.

Aquinas became a lasting and dominant part of the Christian tradition because of his brilliant theological adaptation and commentary on the thought of Aristotle in the context of the complex and incipiently commercial world of his time, the mid-thirteenth century. He was struggling with a challenging new philosophy and engaging with Islamic thought, some of his propositions condemned by the Archbishop of Paris in 1277. So he is not a complete stranger to us. Thomism, the tradition derived from his thought, uses his optimistic account of good and evil – forged in the flames of the Catharist heresy – as a fundamental key to understanding what it means to be human.[17]

His major work, the monumental *Summa Theologiae*, was an extraordinary ethical synthesis from which many have directly drawn. It has informed much Christian thought down the ages. We still live with and debate the just war theory that he developed after Augustine. But the tradition also produced some stultifying misunderstandings of Aquinas' insights: the primary purpose of things, including human sexuality, became crudely 'read off' their physical or biological functioning – not at all his dynamic understanding of the matter.

As might be expected, Thomism presents the true object of human happiness, ultimate human perfection, as being with God, with the 'beatific vision' as the end and purpose (finis), final goal, of human existence.[18] The magnetic North of Thomist thought may have shifted around over the ages but it has remained irreducibly religious.

The risk, of course, is that the 'secular' reader now skips the following pages. They are welcome to do so but they will lose out. For Aquinas understands the human moral quest as involving a trajectory that entails the fulfilment of a 'natural' human happiness, and has a great deal to say about it. In the *Summa*, begun in 1266, he devoted a vast section to 'natural happiness', the integral human fulfilment to which we can aspire in our lifetimes. 'Natural law' is the key to this happiness, what our human reason is there to discover – a common human inheritance which the Christian Church merely articulates.

Animal rights activists please note. Human beings differ from animals, Aquinas concluded, in that they desire *rationally* their specific – species – natural 'good', not 'automatically' or instinctively like a bird covering their eggs. Humanity apprehends the good and acts accordingly – when the just man 'acts in God's eye what in God's eye he is', as the poet Gerald Manley Hopkins put it, in a succinct summary of what Aquinas meant by human nature. What is *reasonable* for human actions and communities is natural to humanity in a way comparable to what is *usual* in the animal kingdom.[19] But, as D. H. Lawrence lamented, men are not as much men as snakes are snakes. The role of reason in ethics invariably entails a defective performance. In other words, we often get it wrong, both in reasoning and moral action.

CAPABILITIES AND VIRTUES

Now acting with moral understanding is a practical matter. In our lifetime ideally we refine our means of learning and choosing those voluntary actions – individual or shared – conducive to a variety of 'goods': our individual good, that of our family, civil society, and the state.[20] We gain in moral experience. This requires schooling – or training and formation – in what today we would probably call moral 'skills' – though skills can be used for good or evil and 'virtues' not. But like playing the piano, virtues also need to be practised with constancy. A virtuous person depends on his or her ability to enjoy doing the right thing, and this develops from success-fully establishing the 'habit' of wanting what will make them truly happy. Exercising acts of 'will-power' against our desires is distinctly second best, literally undesirable.[21]

So, Aquinas did not propose that getting to happiness involves a set of subjective claims – not even the successful claiming of 'human rights' – but a set of objective moral practices; far less the winning of a series of 'issues' – though the *Summa* repeatedly argues all sides of issues. To make a contemporary comparison, Aquinas' under-standing of 'human development' would be analogous to the key insight of the celebrated Indian developmentalist, Amartya Sen: the progressive acquisition of objective capabilities is the nub of the developmental process.[22] This depends on being capable of moral formation, the cultivation of 'virtues', learnt in a lifetime of practice, enabling the choice, priority and allocation of 'values' to happen.

Virtues for Aquinas are 'perfections by which the reason is directed (*ordinatur*) towards God and the lower powers are exercised in accord with the rule of reason'.[23] Above all, the idea that human life has a direction that goes beyond itself, is transcendent, places Aquinas in another country from the western secular world. But to follow this compass bearing, irrespective of the final destination, virtues are universally 'available'.

Aquinas – and Dante – believed that we need to develop at least four capabilities: fortitude, temperance, justice and prudence. Each virtue is significantly different in scope and function, but all are needed for human fulfilment and a just political order. Their meaning and significance for Aquinas is markedly different from what the words evoke today. For example, 'temperance' is best explained as how to enjoy the objects of desires, food, drink and sex, for example, as goods in themselves. Not enjoying them very much can be just as much a vice, *and* self-destructive, as enjoying their effects too much.[24]

What human beings desire is often directed by passions: fear, anger, and sexual attraction. Nothing wrong with these if they are humanised – used in right measure – by the affective virtues of fortitude and temperance. So for the philosopher Jean Porter, the affective virtues should be deployed in accordance with a reasoned grasp of 'what promotes, and what hinders, her attainment of the true human good . . . evaluated primarily in terms of their congruity to the well-being of the agent herself'.[25] Evaluated in other words in terms of solid, old-fashioned self-interest – inclusive of, and not opposed to, the common good. When the passions are lined up in this way behind, for example, work for justice, the individual is on the way to 'natural fulfilment'. This fulfilment is not something other than, or on another path from, the quest for justice and for God.

The moral life is, of course, mostly directed to the concrete problems of what is the right thing to do to, and for, others. This brings into play the lynchpin of Aquinas' ethics – justice. The quest for justice forms the highest form of the ethical life and our use of reason. Note this is not the same as our distinction between head and heart for reason lies at the heart of being human and for Aquinas had echoes of spirituality. So the daily enactment of the common good and thus the creation of the just society, the practice of politics, how to live happily in human communities, lies at the heart of ethics.

A discussion of justice takes up more than half of Aquinas' treatment of the moral virtues in the *Summa*, and he also includes it in sections dealing with the action of God. The just act for Aquinas 'renders what is due'.[26] This is not some subjective judgement like how much to give the refuse collector on Boxing Day, but lies in an objective measure outside the individual, and originates ultimately in the love of God. Justice is thus about how to value people correctly, as God does. So justice cannot be a matter primarily of the emotions, even of compassion – which is transitory – but of willed actions directed towards others and towards human flourishing in society. It is constitutive of society. The yardstick for justice is 'when an individual's actions preserve the relationships of mutual equality which characterise the just community'.[27] So fat-cat salaries are pure injustice. Lining up the emotions behind just actions, tempering them with courage and perseverance, anger at injustice, and compassion for victims forms the practice of what today is called 'solidarity'.

The most intellectual of the virtues is the all-encompassing 'supervirtue' of prudence, the art of moral judgement, not in the sense of taking the right decision – that is the outcome – but of knowing what virtue to deploy in a given situation, and how. Prudence might best be called 'good sense' or discernment, and definitely not 'caution'. It is primarily concerned with settling the means to achieve moral ends. This 'skill' of practical judgement necessarily involves detecting the moral significance of situations and thus their deeper relationship to an ultimate good and happiness. It is most obviously linked to experience and what is normally referred to as wisdom. Given the ethical importance of politics for Aquinas, it is not surprising that he sees statesmanship and the use of practical reason for the common good as the highest form of prudence.[28]

The four cardinal virtues may seem arcane and alien. Indeed they are to many people. But they are arguably the necessary tools of sociability and harmonious relationships. Modernity prefers to theorise and categorise the negative: the pathology of human behaviour, the imperfections of cells and molecules, how things go wrong and defy 'progress'. Study of management techniques is fast becoming the last approved secular forum for approaching the positive idea of virtue: how to get human relationships right, 'me' and 'we', mastering the 'self'. Virtues in Aquinas suggest dynamic qualities needed for what today might be called 'integrity', or in the words of Pope Paul VI, 'integral human development'. The core and dynamics of the latter is what the *Summa* implicitly outlines.

THE SPIRITUALITY OF POLITICS

Aquinas adopts and 'Christianises' Aristotle's ethical insight that political theory represents the highest 'end' of unaided human reason. This does not mean that grand ethical theories that encompass politics make better people. Nor would Aquinas have valued an endless round of interminable and vacuous political meetings. It does mean that the point of building political community is none other than the human good, a vision that can be actively shared by people of all faiths and none. This in no way detracts from the importance given by Aquinas to self-love, by which he meant pursuing 'the fundamental inclinations of human life in a way that respects their intrinsic ordering'.[29] Nor is justice, the practice of politics, pushed upstairs to become overwhelmingly the responsibility of the state – though historically this is exactly what happens to the idea of 'distributive' justice, the allocation of values, wealth and resources, in later centuries – but it is seen as a common responsibility to establish right relationships between people.

Thus the individual and common good stand in a reciprocal relationship; the good of the individual is intrinsic to the common good, and the common good is for the benefit of the individual. 'No one must do harm to another unjustly in order to promote the common good,' he wrote.[30] His is not a mandate for a Christian version of collectivism. He is quite clear that the well-being of individuals and families within a polity are constitutive of the common good not subordinate to it.

The insights stemming from Aquinas' synthesis, though theoretical, have a clarity and practical common-sense quality. Institutions in society, for example, have primary purposes given to them by human beings that should not be subverted. 'That is what it is for' is thus a moral argument. The purpose of the state is primarily to provide the necessary preconditions for the human good, particularly protection of individuals and application of the law. Nothing totalitarian here. Human law 'does not put forward precepts about anything other than justice ... if it prescribes acts of other virtues this is only because and in so far as they take on the character of justice'.[31] The purpose of education is that 'citizens are brought up to preserve the common good of justice and peace'.[32] When the law is subverted and these protections are absent, the political community simply ceases to have any legitimate claim on the allegiance of its members, as it no longer fulfils its purpose.

Aquinas reiterates much of the Church view of his day about the nature and purpose of private property. He makes a common distinction between acquisition and administration versus use. Collective approaches to managing property are ruled out because, in his experience, they simply do not work. They lead to dispute and discord and so should be avoided. But he retains much of the early Church thought about the importance of the shared *use* of property, and the availability of the common goods of the earth for those in need, as might be expected for someone writing towards the end of feudalism. The state can seize property to maintain the life of the community, as may individuals for their survival under certain circumstances such as starvation. The common good is sacred, not ownership of private property.

The *theological* virtues, faith, hope and charity, those given by the grace of God alone, take the trajectory of the good to its limits, making the journey across the inexpressible gulf between the human and God. 'It is only through the theological virtues', Jean Porter writes, 'and especially charity, that women and men are enabled to achieve that inner harmony and unity of life that all things naturally desire.'[33] To dissect out the religious and theological from the political dimension of Aquinas' ethics does damage to the totality of his thought.

ECONOMICS AS IF PEOPLE MATTER

Brick upon brick, Aquinas constructed a logical, and from a Christian perspective, compelling moral framework from the Aristotelian and Augustinian thought of his day. Man is a social animal. Every man is goal-seeking. 'Man discovers and acts out such relationships as are adapted to his searching out his goal with others in fairness to all.'[34]

This logical construction at times is a stumbling block in its rigour. What is *logically* entailed by the nature of money and its transfer lies behind Aquinas' rejection of usury, though he accepts a share of the profits in a joint enterprise or payment as indemnity for losses. And yet we would do well in a world dominated by capital flows to step back and reconsider what has become of money as exchange-value, and what has become of the use-value of products. Does then his view of the world give us answers to the taxing problems of today's globalisation?

Well, obviously not. That would be too easy. And to return to a refined medievalism would be quixotic. The Catholic Church tried it in the 1930s and nearly fell into fascism. The structured discourse of a thirteenth-century theologian and the limits of the political structures of the day are both, in different ways, impediments. His treatment of equity and the role of the state in distributive justice, two of the most pressing political questions today, reflect the limited contemporary possibilities of his society and the early state. The limits to the range of moral problems confronting a Dominican friar, albeit from an aristocratic family linked to the imperial court and well versed in the intrigues of the day, must be acknowledged.

But as a broad framework and way of thinking about human development, and as a means of reintegrating ethics and politics on a firm basis, then surely yes, this offers a starting point. It removes several major contemporary obstacles to thinking coherently and subverts the binary oppositions that we have constructed. It cuts back the undergrowth of an overgrown discourse of human rights. It offers a moral canvas on which to analyse the political economy of globalisation and how to be human in it. His founding of ethics in the virtues chimes with integral human development as the pursuit of, and realisation of, capabilities. Above all it raises the question of what political arrangements of state, civil society and family might be generated by future virtuous citizens – and vice-versa.[35]

Aquinas' thought provokes new tasks for today and offers some tools to tackle them. I would not want to define these tasks very differently from Schumacher's famous phrase 'economics as if people mattered', except to add to it 'politics as if the poor mattered'.[36] They might be shared one day by people of all faiths and none. That is an awful lot better than accepting the political impotence of post-modernism. On the modest grounds that for the starving an old loaf is better than no loaf at all, it will inform indirectly much of the book and I will return to it in the last chapter. But first some empirical facts about the systemic poverty that lies on the dark underside of globalisation.

CHAPTER 3

THE DARK UNDERSIDE
OF GLOBALISATION

A plane lands in the jungle clearing. In a brief encounter between two worlds, diamonds and heroin are taken on and weapons and whisky are taken off. At the official airport outside the capital, World Bank officials disembark, with the staff of the UN agencies and Red Cross in attendance. They bring prescriptions for the other, official economy, the one economists write about. A few nuns with the suffering of their parishioners etched on old faces wait to get on. A little distant, cargo planes fly in with the bounty of the industrialised world for the rich few. Soldiers man the perimeter where goats roam free.

In the capital the national bank stands proud and tall above the tree line, like some Inca temple, with computers and well fed staff, plugged into the outside world, though some of the clerks are thin and will die of AIDS. In the villages nothing seems to have changed for decades, except the transistors and messages on the cast-off T-shirts, the name on the bottled beer, the lost hopes. Hungry women and children walk miles for water, and the old men sit and wait. I think back to an old friend's description of South Africa's apartheid: sin made visible.

It is hard to erase memories of Africa when thinking about poverty in Europe. And increasingly in the last decade NGOs have been highlighting the links between poverty here and poverty there. What is the common denominator? Clearly we are experiencing different instances of the global economy and its shadow-lands. There is the recurrent sense of people abandoned, caught in a closing snare.

'Poverty fetters people socially and psychologically, as well as materially,' writes the British urban sociologist Hilary Russell. 'It goes beyond the lack of physical resources. It can mean being trapped.' The trap springs firmly shut when there are no democratic or legal means of escape. Most particularly, as in many Third World countries, when there is an absence of pro-poor political parties. Or worse – when a political economy of corruption sounds the death-knell to human development. 'Bad governance' is not simply a technical problem.

Of course, people caught in a trap may have all the failings of those who set it. Those caught are easily romanticised, or feared, as victims. One of the things I discovered in the world of development agencies was that, for the best of reasons, the 'entrapments' of poverty were rarely talked about in the same breath as crime and corruption.[1] For such was the not-so-hidden discourse of the Right which saw criminality only as the product of a lack of moral respon-sibility amongst the poor. At the risk of being misunderstood, I have to say that both approaches are mistaken. Criminality is a systemic consequence of the failure to distribute wealth equitably.

THE CONTOURS OF CORRUPTION

Power is entrusted by citizens to governments and to the rule of law for one reason only: so that states may function in the interests of their peoples. Weaker states have considerably less ability to do so in a globalising economy. When power is routinely misused for private gain, such trust is misplaced. Then notions of lawful activity tend to become redundant, and trust is invested in alternative social group-ings and sub-national structures. Under these conditions, society is organised around personal relationships of mutual interest, family and clientship networks, based mainly on religious, ethnic or regional identities. Security, credit, information and making a living depend on belonging to sub-national groupings competing for scarce resources, in the worst cases through violent means, crime and armed conflict.

One of the features of poverty is therefore that high levels of violence and crime contribute to a profound lack of security and opportunity. Yet crime also promises ways out. A sharp drugs dealer on the street can earn as much as a broker in the City. For many, there is no other obvious exit strategy.

Migration out of the 'black holes' of the global economy, like the African country in the first paragraph, more often than not involves migrant strategies that 'host' governments increasingly define as illegal or criminal. Governments' attribution of illegality or criminality to people entering developed countries, other than causing anxiety, high costs and inconvenience when crossing a border, often carries little weight with the migrant. This is for the simple reason that most are escaping societies where the normal expectation is that authority is corrupt. So the question of legality or illegality is redundant, or dealt with by recurrent household expenditure. Just as you bribe your way around soldiers at roadblocks at home, so you pay criminal gangs and traffickers to cross borders abroad. In many low-income countries – and not only in these – crime in the form of corruption is endemic, part of the texture of society.[2]

The economic impact of the misuse of entrusted power becomes more acute when there are high-value goods in play in the economy thanks to extractive industries, like oil, diamonds, timber and gold. Or when defence procurement is a prominent item in the country's national budget and controlled by unaccountable military elites – claims that national security demands secrecy provide the military with an important means of hiding corrupt transactions. Or when rapid privatisation releases valuable state assets into the hands of predatory elites. This was the proximate cause of the partial transformation of the Russian state into a criminal syndicate after the collapse of the Soviet Union. Such criminalisation of Russian state power in addition continues to have very serious implications for nuclear proliferation and the illegal weapons trade, as tens of thousands of military and underpaid workers in the nuclear industry are given every incentive to traffic in nuclear materials and weapons.

Corrupt polities based on clientship are easy prey for criminals. Organised crime swoops like vultures on a decaying body politic to feed on newly available sources of wealth. 'Once the rot has set in, it is virtually unstoppable', Nicky Oppenheimer recently told the Commonwealth Business Forum in Johannesburg, 'until the entire fabric of economic and social development has been completely eroded.'[3] Power then comes to lie in the hands of small criminal, military and political oligarchies whose wealth is stashed overseas and whose power comes from the barrel of a gun. One of the worst recent examples was the former Nigerian head of state, General Sani Abacha, who stole an estimated US \$4.3 billion, half of it from the Nigerian central bank. Only US \$1.4 billion has been found and frozen.

The behaviour of states falls into a spectrum of dereliction with Nigeria and Angola, for example, at one end and the Scandinavian states at the other. Different kinds of predatory states are just as much a feature of the global landscape as the democratic and developmental states that direct investment to productive sectors of the economy and, to some degree, make efforts to sponsor the realisation of the full potential of their citizens. The correlation between the developmental state and democratic practice does not always hold, as illustrated in the authoritarian example of Singapore. Indeed, states such as Mexico have shown features of the clientship-patrimonial, democratic and developmental models at different times in their history.

The degree to which the nascent global economy has provided an unprecedented stimulus to organised crime and corruption is often neglected. Criminal groups have been able to scale up their operations and assert their own unique kind of control over security, credit, information and production, in competition with the state in the new context of the network society. The capacity of organised crime to distance itself from its vast revenues and realise its ill-gotten gains through the financial flows of the global economy, in complex money laundering, has been enhanced by globalisation. Estimates vary from US \$500 billion to US \$1.5 trillion laundered annually. Reactive interventions of nation-states in the market, for example by making trading in drugs and body-parts illegal, banning unauthorised logging, and imposing frontier blocks on migration, ironically provide major opportunities for criminal gain. Crime, like legitimate business, has become globalised and is seizing new opportunities as they present themselves.

Internet paedophile crime gives frightening intimations of future crime in a globalised world. The electronic imaging of the sexual abuse of minors enables pictures to be carried around the world on criminally organised websites. Paedophiles pay to enter the web site with money transferred in symbolic form – also through the use of information technology – by credit card companies. The crime takes place entirely in cyberspace. Except that the destroyed lives of the abused children, and the thousands of men – 7,000 detected in the UK at the time of writing – who have paid to see these images and imagine the reality they convey, exist in real time and space.

In short, organised crime, big and small, has burgeoned in the shadows of globalisation, creating its own networks, finding new openings. The sociologist of the network society, Manuel Castells, is apocalyptic in his assessment. 'The question is', he wrote five years ago, 'not whether our societies will be able to eliminate the criminal networks, but, rather, whether criminal networks will not end up controlling a substantial share of our economy, of our institutions, and of our everyday life.'[4] The jury is out as far as the remnants of the Soviet Union are concerned.

The state is not an incidental nuisance for organised crime, an externality in its niche economics. The entrepreneurs of organised crime depend on corrupting government and state officials, and drawing them into their networks. These were the techniques of the Colombian Cali cartel and the Mexican drugs cartels, which indirectly led to the defeat of the government of President Salinas of Mexico in 1994. Even in Brazil, the State of Espirito Santo illustrates a close linkage between state officials and drugs barons, owing to the reluctance of the federal government to investigate fully.[5]

In other instances the proceeds of organised crime, or other illegal activity, are used to fund political parties against future favours. Corruption runs from high officials to minor civil servants. And 'high officials' include several heads of state. In the period 2000–2002, Indonesia's President, Abdurahman Wahid, Thailand's Thaksin Shinawatra, Joseph Estrada of the Philippines, Carlos Menem of Argentina, Arnoldo Alemán of Nicaragua, India's Prime Minister P. V. Narsimha Rao, and the Chief Justice of Malta were all under investigation for corrupt practice. In the last two decades, it is calculated, some $20 billion were siphoned into Swiss bank accounts by African heads of state.

But the developed world cannot congratulate itself on probity, least of all after the financial scandals that have recently rocked the USA. The collapse of Enron and WorldCom in 2002 revealed how fragile business ethics were in the smartest of US trading companies. And it takes two to tango. Offers of bribes often come from companies based in democratic countries that – implausibly – try to assume the moral high ground. The investigations into the notorious French Elf Aquitaine affair – the then state-owned oil company – that initially resulted in the conviction of the then French Foreign Minister, Roland Dumas, on 30 May 2001, revealed that the company had sent US $77.1 million to Swiss bank accounts for 'execution of Elf Group commitments', widely thought to be kickbacks for the Angolan and Francophone African heads of state. The NGO Global Witness describes the Elf Aquitaine affair as 'a gruesome tale of money laundering and state robbery at the expense of the long-suffering Angolan people'.[6]

It is difficult to quantify how much this type of corruption costs struggling developing countries but it runs into billions of dollars. The former head of Pakistan's Accountability Bureau, now wound up, claimed in October 2000 that senior military officers had taken $1 billion in kickbacks during the preceding years for eight major defence contracts. Estimates of corruption by state officials in the new capitalist China put the cost to the state of their crime at anything between 3–16% of the country's GDP. This level of drain on the public purse has to be considered as a key factor in explaining why sustainable development in a global economy is so difficult.[7]

These rough guides give no indication of the debilitating impact of predatory bureaucracies on the private purse and the entrepreneurial spirit of citizens. While the newsworthy arrest of top officials and presidents is shocking, their gross misdemeanours are but the more visible aspect of the wider problem of corruption. Once part of the texture of society, corrupt state officials and bureaucracy at every level use their control of state assets and positions to raise 'rents' or bribes. So corruption involves both high state officials acting as corrupt gatekeepers for the foreign businesses wishing to penetrate a country's economy, and underpaid minor state officials, milking citizens. The latter make their money by seeking 'rents' from citizens trying to gain access to basic services and utilities. Ports and courts, pensions and hospitals, dealing with police and prison officers, with soldiers and border controls, all are occasions when citizens commonly have to bribe an individual.

The cost of bribes for getting past officials and moving goods through ports forms in many parts of the developing world a vast disincentive – a negative subsidy – for export production, undermining prospects for small-scale industrialisation. Corruption at the

Bangladesh port of Chittagong, it is estimated, costs the country £1.1 billion per annum. Productive forms of foreign direct investment (FDI) simply will not flow into countries such as Bangladesh, widely seen as one of the worst in the world for corruption. Illegal logging in Cambodia loses the state some 90% of the revenue it might expect from its legal timber trade. Economists estimate that the losses due to corruption in Brazil – by no means a predatory state – amount to US $6,000 per person per annum, about fifteen times the income of the poorest 10% of its citizens. An African producer may have to pass so many corrupt soldiers and officials in order to export his goods that his profit has disappeared before they have got onto a ship. Legitimate business is made impossible and public office is undermined.

By the late 1990s the problem of corruption moved centre stage in the development debate as donor governments, following the logic of liberalisation, tried to promote export-led development using this as an excuse for retrenching aid budgets. For every $100 of its state expenditure the USA was giving some 10 cents for development aid, and most of this went to strategic allies such as Egypt or Israel. Large-scale 'development' projects in key sectors such as water and power, dams and hydroelectric schemes, requiring procurement and deals with contractors, offered multiple opportunities for corruption in 'gatekeeper states'. Many governments liked them. For example, the US $8 billion Lesotho Highlands Water Project in Lesotho provided a string of construction contracts and, by June 2001, with a certain inevitability, the head of the Lesotho Highlands Water Authority was up in court facing corruption charges dating back to 1986. No wonder many governments encouraged large projects and some aid donors have begun to fear them.

It is but a short journey from predatory states to *collapsed* states where any meaningful governance has ceased to exist. The lure of mineral wealth not only stimulates corruption but, far worse, fuels 'war economies' in parts of Africa. By this is meant a cycle of accumulation and violence by armed sub-national units often in order to control and sell valuable mineral resources, such as 'conflict diamonds', to pay for more weapons. Foday Sankoh's rebel forces in Sierra Leone had one major interest, the control of diamond deposits whose sale was organised through neighbouring Liberia under President Charles Taylor. In response, the Sierra Leonian regime invited in mercenary forces to protect it from the rebels in exchange for diamond concessions. This was why the majority of people welcomed an armed British intervention.

The internationalising of African wars has relied on Faustian pacts of this sort. The vicious patrimonial regime of the Kabilas in the Congo drew in the armies of neighbouring countries using the mineral bait. In July 1999 Laurent Desiree Kabila signed away 25 years' exclusive rights over the two rich diamond deposits in Mbuji-Mayi from the majority state-run Societé Minière de Bakwanga (MIBA) to a shady Zimbabwean company, Sengamines, in a deal amounting to several billion US dollars. Some of the profits went to senior Zimbabwean military officers, and probably to the head of Zimbabwean State Security, Emmerson Mnangagwa. One of the Zimbabwean mining companies involved, OSLEG, 'Operation Sovereign Legitimacy' – as Goebbels said the best lies are the biggest – had amongst its directors a Zimbabwean lieutenant general and a permanent secretary in the Ministry of Defence, plus the head of the Zimbabwean Minerals Marketing Corporation. Another player, Oryx Zimcon, registered in the Cayman Islands, was also a joint Zimbabwean Defence Force owned company.[8]

The developmental consequences of such wars hardly need underlining. Despite vast natural resources of gold, uranium, cobalt, coltran – one of its components titanium is used in electronics – copper, timber and water, the Congo lies 155th out of 173 countries, almost at the bottom of the UN human development league tables. Only small criminal cliques holding high civilian or military office have benefited significantly from its vast national wealth.

The growing criminality that has taken root in the developing world has played into the hands of anti-aid lobbyists who, for a variety of reasons, want aid to be reduced. Public perceptions of a 'bottomless pit', money 'getting into the wrong hands', have made it harder to argue the continued importance of aid flows. This is another reason why international NGOs (INGOs) have been reluctant to burden themselves by making the running on corruption, though privately recognising it as an impediment to development. The weight has been borne largely by Transparency International in Berlin, set up as an INGO specifically with this mandate, putting pressure on governments for reform, and producing an annual audit of countries around the world.

The response of the World Bank to corruption has been to try to circumvent gatekeeper officials at a national level, by promoting 'de-centralisation', the euphemism for avoiding the centralised predatory state. But the bubble in the wallpaper has simply moved, often opening up new problems by reinforcing the power of corrupt local authorities. Northern ministries of development assistance have begun differentiating a 'deserving' from an 'undeserving poor' by selecting countries based on criteria of low corruption levels and commitment to equitable and sustainable development. INGOs insist that their mode of operation in NGO-to-NGO funding, with careful monitoring and frequent hands-on visiting, offers more safeguards while not being 100% corruption proof.

The culture of bribes, kickbacks and 'protection' is the dominant one for much of the hinterland of globalisation. It is the antithesis of development. Corruption has contributed to a stagnating or collapsing standard of living for countless numbers of people around the world while small minorities have accumulated extraordinary wealth. For most Africans, public services and institutions are synonymous with corruption and low standards. That the management of public funds lacks transparency is assumed to be the normal state of affairs. The danger is that this becomes a self-fulfilling prophecy with punitive action contributing to a reduction in the state's legitimacy rather than reform and encouragement of new pro-poor political movements and parties.

This culture, and the politics of the belly that goes with it, works on the premise of violence as the natural order of things. It grows out of an experience of reckless and despairing urgency. Trying to escape from the trap of locality and poverty ends up in a variety of blind alleys: drugs, both supply and demand, the solidarity of gangs, trafficking in people, women and children and body parts, making a living from the gun. For some of the wretched of the earth, insertion into the network of organised crime becomes the goal and meaning of life in a globalised world.

DRUGS IN THE SHADOW-LANDS

The drugs trade can only fully be understood in this context. It is a form of survival strategy, for a few a way out, and also, to some degree, a perverse form of resistance. In Colombia the sugar market and textile industry collapsed in the 1980s as synthetic fibres came in and sugar prices dropped. Industrialisation failed. This left marijuana, and later cocaine production, as an attractive production alternative. A family in Chapare in Bolivia harvesting four crops of coca leaves a year can hope to earn an income of US $20,000 from buyers from the drugs cartels. With coffee halving in price in the last two years and worth far less than coca leaves per kilo, there is simply no comparison in household income between producing for a legal and impoverishing trade and for an illegal and enriching one. Farmers can and do use this money in an economically rational way by building decent accommodation instead of shacks, and buying transport to move produce, and people, to town and markets. Once coca is processed into cocaine, a kilo in 1990s Colombia was worth US $750, though, by the time it was cut and sold on the streets of the USA and Europe, this rose to US $135,000.[9]

The geographical configuration of value-added – from raw coca leaf into paste, to cocaine and then cut, or turned into crack – is a spectacular instance of the mark-up made on other primary commodities that move from the developing into the industrialised world. Though in the drugs trade asymmetric profit is exaggerated because of legal constraints on supply, it is typical of the unfair trade between the First and Third World. Most of the value is realised outside Latin America and Asia. But in this instance, the high value nature of the final manufactured product allows countless farmers to make a modest living at the price of a semi-clandestine and precarious life.

At the other end of the scale, criminal profits from the trade amount to some US $500 billion, more than that of the oil companies in 1994, and by now a key element in the economies of Mexico and a number of other countries. Those responsible for the management of the trade are sub-national groups based on ethnicity or other forms of shared experience – the Russian Mafias started in the gulags. The Yakuza of Japan, the Sicilian Cosa Nostra, the Russian Mafias and Jamaican Yardies form competitive, but sometimes collaborative, networks around the world. They link up locally with small fry criminals – and sometimes with political parties – and globally through offshore banks, which launder their money.[10]

The contours of the drugs trade highlight the global patchwork of the apartheid of poverty. It is a concentrated expression of the dynamics engendered by the economic policies of the 1980s that so accelerated globalisation. Deprived urban areas are the centres of drug supply and small-scale criminal drugs distribution. They are the forcing ground for criminality and violence, producing in the USA the majority of the 5.4 million Americans who are under some sort of legal constraint, prison, probation or parole, 2.8% of the total population. In 2002 the USA prison population exceeded two million for the first time, a per capita incarceration rate of 697 per 100,000 of the population – compared with 127 per 100,000 in England and Wales.[11]

As might be expected given the disproportionate percentage of poor black families living in deprived urban areas, the figures are sharply racially differentiated: 12% of African-Americans aged 20–34, the highest rate ever recorded, were in US jails in 2002 compared to 1.6% of Whites; 40% of the people on death row were black and most of these will be judicially killed by the state. California, with its Silicon Valley, saw a fourfold increase in its number of prisons in the 1980s; 40% of its young black population has been under some form of criminal justice constraint at some time in their lives. Nationally a stunning 28% of black men will spend some time in prison in the USA during their lifetime. Moreover the life expectancy of young black men is less than that of a comparable age group in communist China. It is perhaps not surprising that the USA, the major driving force of contemporary globalisation, shows such a stark differentiation in the lives and well-being of 'high value, low value and no value' people and places, a pattern exported around the world.[12]

TRAFFICKING IN PEOPLE

There is a perennial temptation to demonise or romanticise the cultures of poverty that produce such statistics. One of the features of life in the shadow-lands of today's powerful networks dominated by finance capital – reminiscent in many ways of the period of early industrialisation in Britain – is a resurgence of violence against women and children. A few figures selected at random give some idea. Recorded maltreatment of children in the lowest income families in the USA saw a sharp rise in the 1980s; by 1993, if the records show real trends not increased reporting, children of such families were eighteen times more likely to be sexually abused and twenty-two times more likely to be badly physically maltreated than the average American child. Looking at the global treatment of children, the International Labour Organisation (ILO) calculates that there are 250 million child workers around the world, 153 million in Asia working under deplorable conditions in everything from carpet weaving to brick making to domestic service. The incidence of child soldiers is growing. Figures for violence against women show similar increases. The incidence of rape is South African townships and in rural Eastern Congo is high enough to be described as a humanitarian crisis.

This resurgence of violence against the defenceless is part of a much larger recent change in the lives of women and children. The economic crises of the last three decades – for example the 1973–4 oil shock – have demanded cost savings from businesses. Skilled women's labour is obtained at far lower cost than men's, and women's employment has grown exponentially. Many children in the Third World – and to a smaller extent in the First World – are drawn or pushed into supplementing meagre family incomes as even lower-cost labour in family-run and small national enterprises.

There has also been the perennial push factor of families needing the income earned by women in their fight against relative or absolute poverty. Mainly in the developed world, the social status, sociability and institutional belonging that come from waged employment should also be taken into account. The rise of feminism has interacted with higher levels of employment opportunities for women and, together with increased purchasing power and in-dependence, has significantly eroded the dominance of the patriarchal family. This in turn has had knock-on effects in the negotiation of authority throughout all social institutions.

The interpretation and explanation of these changes have formed key thematic elements in the political discourse of Right and Left, liberal and conservative, each with different diagnoses of the dis-contents of gender, structural transformation and globalisation. All, however, might sign on to the proposition that the structure of the patriarchal family has been crumbling without anything viable to put in its place, whether arising from new family patterns in civil society, or provided by the state. And perhaps most would also concur that this contributes to the destruction of the traditional defensive and protective bastion – however defective – to the exploitation of children. In Rio's drugs gangs alone there are estimated to be more than 6,000 Brazilian 'child soldiers', aged between 10 and 18 – this at a time when the concept of childhood is under sustained attack from sex tourism, child pornography and the definition of childhood and youth as a vital part of a segmented consumer market.[13] It does not require a rosy view of the patriarchal family, and its own sometimes violent history, to suggest that nothing has replaced it as a site of cultural and moral formation, with negative consequences particularly for children.

Estimates of the number of child prostitutes in the USA and Canada combined vary from 100,000 to 300,000. In Thailand the figure may be as high as 800,000, with India not far behind. Some are sold to pimps, others kidnapped, others trafficked across borders. The Yakuza specialise in trafficking children into adoption rings for childless couples in the USA at c. US $20,000 per head, and moving women from Asia into Japanese brothels. This is not to say that child prostitution is directly caused by the breakdown of the patriarchal family, only that extreme poverty finds cultural and moral defences against the exploitation of children increasingly eroded, and past gains in children's rights are now under threat or reversed.[14]

Trafficking in women is even more complex. Here can be detected echoes of the 'white slavery' anxieties of Victorian England, and conversely concern from some feminist groups that sex-workers are misrepresented as helpless victims in order to reinforce male authoritarian attitudes.[15] So it is important to underline that 'trafficking' describes both the recruitment and transport of women for gain, using overt threats or use of force or deception, and the free movement of sex-workers in pursuit of a significant source of income, though even the latter have a high degree of vulnerability. Notwithstanding, many of the latter are tricked into believing conditions of employment and pay will be acceptable to them, and they become the prisoners of pimps, chattels for sale, their labour exploited abusively. Many are effectively in debt bondage, owing fees and inflated travel costs, and in only the most formal sense free agents. The rise of the tourist and entertainment industries has turned prostitution into big business on a global scale.[16]

Trafficking involves, of course, not only sex-workers but also significant numbers of other economic migrants. Most of those trafficked cross borders as undocumented migrants whose pass-ports, if they have one, have been confiscated by their traffickers, or with fake visas and travel documents provided for them. They may die at sea, or in sealed vans, and travel in abject dependency on criminal gangs. Trafficked sex-workers are the worst off: in abusive relationships and intolerable working conditions they are simply too frightened to testify against their pimps. In one study of 234 traf-ficked persons undertaken by the German government, not necessarily all sex-workers, 134 victims, or their families in their countries of origin, had been threatened by their traffickers to stop them testifying against them. But even where prostitution is legal, trafficked sex-workers themselves tend to be treated by police in many countries on a spectrum from low priority 'illegals' to crimi-nals. In countries such as Burma, where women are sent as sex-workers to Thailand, 'a vital node' on the transnational route, or Albania and the Ukraine, which supplies a wide European market, corrupt police link up with criminal gangs. Fear of the stigma of prostitution at home, and of penalties against their families from traffickers, plays an important role in making successful prose-cutions against traffickers the exception.[17]

Trafficking in people is now big business. Profits of traffickers based in the Caribbean and Mexico targeting the lucrative passage to the USA are estimated at c. US $3.5 billion per annum. Trafficking in bits of people is also growing. Body parts such as corneas and kidneys are moved from patchworks of poverty to the rich enclaves of the North, from Latin America to German, Swiss and Italian buyers, and from India and Egypt to the oil-rich of the Middle East. Human 'donkeys' are used in the drugs trade, usually women with drugs secreted on, or in, their bodies. Some seek to escape but many intend to return. Their motivation may be money for their children's medical and educational expenses. The only thing left to sell when poverty has removed all other assets or productive possibilities is the human body.

Government restrictions on inter-state mobility, particularly for unskilled labour, is self-evidently the proximate cause of contem-porary trafficking in people. The criminal gangs who conduct the traffic might be looked on as a privatised version of the state gate-keepers who use their entrusted office for private gain, and for whom the territorial boundaries of states are an opportunity, not an impediment. For some of the lowest income countries, frontiers and their control are amongst the last vestiges of the territorial outreach of states for whom the only other reality is a name-plate in the UN General Assembly room. And trafficking is a perverse – reverse – parasitism on the state's gateways, a rival privatisation of the corrupt benefits accruing from state border controls.

This litany of global misery and affluence may offer a dismal geography of globalisation from the underside. But juxtaposed to information and financial flows and the dominant networked society, this is an important, isolated and vast hinterland. Here is the shadow-land that the chivalric troubadours of the international non-governmental agencies (INGOs) sometimes romanticise, or which their opponents readily code and classify as the heart of darkness, the primary source of the illegality and criminality that threatens the enclaves of the rich. Yet crime has no single source or place.

This dispiriting story can easily be re-interpreted and recoded under a more sober and realistic world image of poverty, setting us off on a different track from punishment and containment, into the demands of a complex interconnected world, the simple demands of justice. A world of people, places and bodies defined and trapped by others and by a global system, it nonetheless cannot be dissociated from the other world of prosperity and consumption in the affluent nodes of the global network. Preyed on by criminal, military and political elites, the poor supply our world with primary products, oil, minerals, cheap skilled labour, bodies and body parts, narcotics, and the fantasy of the exotic and frightening. And in turn they are supplied with weapons, cigarettes, alcohol, surplus food and aid. It does not have to be that way. We do not have to be that way. So how did it come about?

CHAPTER 4

THE GLOBAL
POLITICAL ECONOMY

'When has the entire earth ever been so closely joined by so few threads? Who has ever had more power and more machines such that with a single impulse, with a single movement of a finger, entire nations are shaken . . .?' Not the head of the World Bank speaking, but the reflections of Herder, the German philosopher, in 1774.[1] The background was the great European imperial expansion, accelerating growth in trade, mainly in sugar, tobacco, tea and opium, with companies and missionaries fanning out across the world. Immanuel Kant, writing in the same period, reflected on the new cosmopolitan liberal order growing up, and discussed the prospects for what, today, we would call a 'global civil society'. Both were reacting to an 'internationalisation' of the economy, a process slowed down by the consolidation, then rise, of the nation-state during the nineteenth century.[2]

This chapter tries to tell the story of how today's political economy originated, and the process of globalisation from the top. For the development of interconnected societies, foreshadowing a progressive 'worldwide' integration of national economies, did not begin a few decades ago. By 1900, at the apogee of European imperial outreach, a further wave of economic expansion was in full swing. This was boosted by investment within territories politically controlled by the imperial centre, at the nub of wider linkages to other national economies. It created a modern, open and integrated system for trade in agricultural products and in the new industrial commodities. The dominant power of the nation-state was now the dynamo generating a complex international economy. From 1870 to 1914 trade expanded at an average rate of 3.4% per annum and the share of British wealth invested abroad rose from 17% to 33% – though more of this investment was outside the Empire than within it. Economic expansion was accompanied by a prodigious move-ment of labour out of Europe, some 36 million mainly economic migrants moving to the USA.[3]

Cotton, sugar and coal were now being carried around the world by new – industrialised – means of transport, in steamships. Trade increasingly depended on effective means of fast, real-time com-munication, the intercontinental telegraph and telephone. The economist Maynard Keynes followed his eighteenth-century prede-cessors in reflections on the new economy: he marvelled at the Edwardian Londoner sipping his tea in bed and ordering 'the various products of the whole earth in such quantity as he might see fit' – though by using the 'revolutionary' telephone rather than today's Tesco web site.[4] By the outbreak of the 1914 war some 44% of the capital invested outside nation-states was British owned, double the amount of its nearest rival, France. The economic impact of the First World War, the protectionist tariffs that followed – charging for imports to come into the country, and exchange controls – limiting the flow of capital across national borders, should not be under-estimated; from 1914 to 1950 trade declined to an average rate of expansion of only 1% per annum.[5]

It was later, in the era of decolonisation, that a faltering develop-ment of embryonic global and international institutions – multinational corporations (MNCs) and business houses, the UN system, the World Council of Churches, a genuinely global rather than European Catholic Church – took off. In the immediate after-math of the Second World War, a common perception arose that the power of narrow national self-interest needed to be contained by new institutions that could negotiate the global dimension of inter-national trade and interdependence. Of course, each of the victors saw this as occurring in a way most beneficial to himself. But a period of post-colonial 'globalising' had begun. It took until the mid-1980s for trade as a percentage of GDP (Gross Domestic Product), the measure of trade as an ingredient in national wealth-creation, to reach the same level as before the First World War and to regain its significance. It was at this time that consciousness of globalisation as a process emerged.[6]

The growing power of the multinational corporations (MNCs) was and is acknowledged as the most obvious force building a new globalising economy. Defined simply as corporations controlling assets – factories, mines, marketing offices – in more than two countries, MNCs are major bearers of the 'soft power' that is shaping the structures of a new world. In other words the MNCs get people to want what MNCs want – rather than what they need – without overt coercion.[7] Their manufacturing production chain is dispersed across many countries in small-scale units that increasingly they control rather than own. A constitutive feature of globalisation is that economic activity increasingly takes place, not simply between territorial states but *within multinational corporations*.

GDP and trade rose consistently from 1950 to 1973. The background to this golden era of rising prosperity was strong domestic demand – people kept on spending. Internationally the key was the functioning of the self-regulatory regime, hammered out by the UK and USA and finally approved by the economists of the world powers in July 1944 in the little New Hampshire town of Bretton Woods.[8] Essentially, this tied the exchange value of the US dollar to that of gold, and the rest of the world's currencies to the US dollar. The dollar's link to gold meant that the US government had to pay creditor central banks for its current account deficits with bars of gold, and was constrained to uphold the value of its currency at a fixed rate. The plot of the Ealing Studios' film *The Lavender Hill Mob*, made in this period, involved gentleman crooks accidentally exporting Bank of England gold bars melted down into the shape of Eiffel Towers. If the gold reserves at Fort Knox became too low, this acted as a trigger. Lending by US banks would be cut. As money dried up demand would fall – and with it the volume of imports – thus reducing the deficit. At least that was the theory.

When, in August 1971, President Nixon discovered that he could not both fund Johnson's 'Great Society' anti-poverty programmes and sustain war expenditure in Vietnam, the constraints of Bretton Woods proved too great. He first sought revaluation of the European currencies – this was refused – and then broke the link with gold. Henceforth he was able to handle rising US deficits by printing dollars and issuing Treasury bills in time honoured fashion. The citizens of the USA could comfortably go on consuming more of the world's wealth than they created. The reserves in the world's central banks rose sevenfold during the 1970s as the US pumped out dollars, 'exporting liquidity'. Inflation – too much money chasing too few goods – became entrenched in the world financial system. In net recipient countries credit became cheap, great bursts in domestic credit were made possible, and the way opened for later booms and busts through massive international movements of capital.[9]

Between 1973 and 1974 the OPEC states cartel quadrupled the price of oil and exacerbated the coming problems of excess global liquidity and its resulting inflationary impact. Petro-dollars from the OPEC oil-producing states were piled on top of Euro-dollars. European and US banks recycled them to debtor nations at low interest rates. A debt crisis arose when the US hiked its own interest rate in the early 1980s and interest rates around the world followed suit. Had the post-war UN dispensation been allowed to create more effective international regulatory mechanisms, for example permitting persistent surpluses to be penalised, as well as dealing with deficits, some of this might have been avoided and some of it successfully managed. But the International Monetary Fund (IMF) and World Bank were effectively cut loose from the umbilical cord of the UN system at birth. As a consequence of weighted voting, and by other means, they were soon profoundly influenced by US financial and trade policy, or sometimes simply mistaken in their policy prescriptions. Indeed economic orthodoxy was moving in the opposite direction to the restraints of Bretton Woods. Deregulation was becoming the order of the day.

The 1973–4 oil crisis sharply raised costs of production in the industrialised world by raising energy bills pushing policy-makers into a major restructuring of the global economic system. The Reagan–Thatcher years of the 1980s ushered in a decade that rejected Keynes' insights and espoused a neo-liberal ideology. The export of this ideology resulted in dire short-term consequences around the world: cutbacks in government services, most damaging in health and education, reductions in price support for essential commodities for the poor, wage cuts and increased inequality, leading to riots and social instability.

Overlapping the debt crises, as interest rates soared and debt repayments became impossible, beginning with the Mexican *peso* crisis in 1982, there was the disastrous bursting of capital 'bubbles'. First came Japan's slow and agonising decline beginning in 1990, and then, starting in 1997, the Asian, followed by the Russian and Brazilian crises. After the collapse of the Thai *baht* in July 1997, strong national economies began falling like dominoes with consequences, aggravated by doctrinaire IMF interventions, ranging from damaging to devastating. Large short-term financial flows were acting like tidal waves, breaking down the weakened defences of the relatively resilient 'Tiger' economies, which had been the remarkable success stories of a miserable decade for the developing world, what became known as 'the development disaster of the 1980s'.[10]

The feature of the most recent period of globalisation, emerging clearly by the end of the 1980s, the characteristic that distinguishes it from previous phases of international economic change, thus lies chiefly in a rapid growth of footloose capital and prodigious financial flows. This is traceable to large recurrent US current account deficits, the US government's economic goals, and a set of policies projected globally to achieve them. World trade in services quadrupled between 1980 and 1999 reflecting the growth of institutions profiting, amongst other transactions, from the packaging and management of financial flows in different forms of portfolio investment, short-term capital movements and financial instruments. In the words of the financier, George Soros: 'A plethora of derivatives, synthetic products, and other new financial products were introduced, and the financial landscape changed out of all recognition. That is when globalisation truly took shape.'[11]

In short, today's globalisation is marked by the growing dominance of the finance sector in global economics, aptly dubbed the 'financialisation' of economic life, the rapid increase in the velocity and complexity of transactions in different forms of money, coupled with the reduced cost of communication. This results in stock markets increasingly determining economic stability and growth. It features a major increase in transactions on the bond markets – an important way governments borrow money to plug their budgets – with 14%, some $5 trillion, issued and bought internationally. As a result, almost a quarter of the USA's federal debt was owed to non-residents by 1999, and foreign ownership of UK gilts, long-term government bonds, tripled to 19% between 1980 and 1999. An important element of this expansion in international transactions is the rapid recent rise in the sale of commercial (non-government bonds), 'over the counter (OTC)' trading outside stock exchanges which accounts for trillions of dollars, and daily currency transactions which stood at $1.2 trillion in 2001. The most notable growth has come in foreign direct investment (FDI), the purchase of ownership in foreign companies, and 'greenfield investments', the building of multinational subsidiaries, increasing annually by some 20% between 1985 and 1995.[12]

The casino quality of most financial flows makes FDI superficially appear a financial development beneficial to the poorest nations, and potentially it may be. Technology and expertise may be transferred. But, the only obviously productive form of investment, it is not nearly so productive of economic development as at first sight it appears. Over half FDI represents the economic activity of multinational corporations (MNCs) buying up smaller companies, merging with them or investing as key shareholders in others. Some 60% of this investment takes place between the major industrialised blocs, USA, Europe and Japan. The remaining 40% is highly skewed towards ten Asian countries, including China with its booming Pacific seaboard economy. Africa with 10% of the world's population barely gets 2% of world FDI. In short, at least half the world is not affected significantly by FDI flows.

If the touchstone of recent globalisation is taken to be this *tsunami* wave of financial flows, then it would be true to say that today's globalisation is still not global. Most of Africa, excluding a few countries with significant oil or mineral resources, receives no investment. Africa is thus not integrated into 'the global economy' in any meaningful sense. Nor is it likely to be in the foreseeable future. This uneven and inequitable distribution of capital, determined mainly by investment decisions of the MNCs, calls in question the realism of any theory of economic development that seeks the 'insertion' of the developing world in the global economy, the mantra of European international co-operation.

Furthermore, the common use of the term 'transnational' gives the impression that with MNCs we are dealing with global institutions. But scrutiny of the boards of multinationals, the places where they make the bulk of their profits, and how they operate, shows that they remain essentially regional – at most international – rather than global. They reflect their countries of origin with only those of smaller countries, such as Netherlands and Switzerland, tending towards genuinely international staffing and leadership. As far as production is concerned, most multinationals are mainly regional, spreading production across borders in defined regions rather than globally. That they work predominantly from a national home base still defines their operation today. This is not surprising given the importance of North American multinationals and their vast domestic market. Comparing the Ford motor company and the Roman Catholic Church, only the latter is a transnational acting globally.[13]

Nonetheless, the 60,000 MNCs in existence at the turn of the millennium with their 820,000 foreign subsidiaries are a unique feature of the contemporary international landscape. With a turnover of $15.6 trillion, representing 50% of global GDP and 70% of global trade, their growth in the 1990s has been the key element in internationalising economic transactions. In short, multinationals may become more global in future through mergers and acquisitions of national companies, one of the major components of FDI, through further restructuring of production, and as a result of cultural changes in leadership. But they are not there yet.

The technological basis for the emergence of nascent global institutions like the MNCs lies in the communications and information technology revolutions whose enormous significance became apparent during the 1990s. Developments in microchips and fibre optics drastically reduced the cost of communication, making possible a massive compression of space and time in cyberspace. Most notably the new technology permitted complex manufactured goods to be assembled from components made in a number of different countries and then brought together 'just in time'. A high percentage of 'trade' figures represent components moving about across borders within these large companies. For example, 45% of US exports to Mexico – linked in the NAFTA (North American Free Trade Area) border industries – are now intra-company movements.[14]

The internationalisation of production enables MNCs to maximise their cost savings by exploiting localised skills and cheap labour pools and by using 'transfer pricing' to take advantage of the most favourable tax regimes. Likewise the attraction of major MNC investment and development has prompted nation-states to offer ever more attractive tax and labour conditions in a game of 'beggar my neighbour'. The threat of a downward spiral is never far off. In addition the new information-rich economy enables new forms of company to evolve whose wealth depends on control of production in complex networks involving semi-independent productive units, spread across regions. In a step up from this the big 'logo' companies, such as Nike and Gap, see themselves primarily in the business of marketing what others produce – as cheaply as possible – rather than production itself. Thus not only has the significance of nation-state boundaries changed, but also those of the companies themselves.

The diffusion of economic power at the expense of territorial identities should not, though, be exaggerated. The home-based leadership of MNCs and the national political elites of the developed countries work in close political contact so that MNC lobbying has a powerful impact on government policy. One of the most powerful groups is the Transatlantic Business Dialogue, made up of the chief executive officers of the hundred most powerful EU and US multinationals. US agribusinesses have played a major role in determining US trade policy, making sure their views prevailed in international trade negotiations, by staffing advisory groups of US negotiators. The policies of the present Bush administration are notoriously influenced by the oil lobby.

Perhaps the closest relationship occurs in military production where government export guarantees for domestic arms-production are linked to foreign policy goals and generate a high level of co-ordination. This is reflected in the extraordinary cost to citizens of sustaining the arms industry. It has been calculated that the total subsidy to arms manufacture from government in the UK is £4.25 billion, counting research and development £12,300 for each job in the industry.[15]

So while it may sometimes be convenient for governments to claim that certain aspects of economic policy are simply out of their control because of global financial markets, and, in parenthesis, the power of MNCs, the reality is more complex. Outcomes are negotiated in shifting relationships of power in flexible hierarchies that share considerable mutual interests. The military-industrial complex of the Eisenhower years has evolved into a government-MNC complex involving several departments of state. Top staff shift between the two carrying with them past obligations.

What is palpably out of control is the recurrent creation of capital 'bubbles', as capital pours into a particular country or a sector of its economy. The most recent case of this is the 'irrational exuberance' shown towards the economic potential of cyberspace. The shark frenzy for dot.com and telecom stocks worked itself out from 2001 to 2003 in a major stock market crash, flight from the dollar and incipient global recession. The high level corruption in the Enron and WorldCom corporations added to the tailspin. This has high-lighted the instability of the global economy and its reliance on the USA.[16]

The growing fragility of the international economic architecture has resulted not from some inexorable economic evolution, but from a raft of policy decisions taken by the richer industrialised nations led by the USA. It was, and is, the result of choices and policies, not of blind historical inevitability. And in democracies these choices are ultimately our responsibility. The weakness of regulatory mechanisms and the inadequacy of contemporary forms of economic governance are the result of the contemporary unrivalled projection of both soft and coercive power by the USA. The failure of any effective moderating counter-force, most notably that of the European Union, to engage at a global level is an important contributory cause.

US HEGEMONY: OFFERS YOU CAN'T REFUSE

Globalisation lends itself to inflated claims both negative and positive. Many of the political and economic developments at the heart of globalisation get described in apocalyptic and exaggerated ways. Screaming headlines: 'The End of the Nation State', 'Global Proletarians', 'Welfare States Cannot Survive' add to a sense of local impotence hopelessly contemplating apparent global omnipotence. But it is true that economic policies and events in one place, pre-eminently in the US, have disproportionate effects elsewhere, beyond the immediate control of all but US policy-makers with their power to shape global economic structures.

Control of nation-state economies *is* more difficult in a globalising economy. It is harder to tax capital, for example, because of its mobility. But there are ways of dealing with the problem as Malaysia showed in the Asian crisis when it temporarily locked in capital.

Welfare states can fund welfare in a variety of ways and in a variety of forms, and have done, and have survived. As for 'global proletarians', globalisation creates differentiated workforces and consumer groups, areas of productive wealth and areas of desperate poverty; it can preserve and encourage diversity.[17] Dealing with diversity is the stock in trade of the modern corporation. Nonetheless, a surprising number of critics are happy to frolic in the mists of ideology and contemporary mythology, avoiding the mundane messiness of history. One consequence is a time-consuming diversion of analysis into blind alleys. Another is that key political questions are ducked.

Perhaps the most unproductive debate to date revolves round whether globalisation is an inevitable process or a colossal conspiracy: whether we observe and forecast it like the weather or see it as emerging from a coherent and powerful group of agencies. The latter gives an unrealistic account of the coherence of power in the contemporary world. Globalisation is a historical process engendered by specific policies arising from specific beliefs and a distinctive conceptual mapping. Only its technological underpinning is irreversible. In short, it is a political economy. Moreover, its development in theory and practice as an ideology cannot be dissociated from the changing role of the USA as it morphs from superpower to what the French call a *hyperpuissance*, hyperpower.[18]

It is in the nature of economic theories that they are akin to beliefs, and generate quasi-religious levels of commitment in an international priesthood of learned believers. During the 1980s the Reagan and Thatcher administrations converted to 'market fundamentalism'. They set out to 'knock down barriers', free up trade and liberalise economies for different forms of foreign investment. They contributed to making the creed of neo-liberalism – an amalgam of privatisation, fiscal austerity and reheated nineteenth-century trade liberalism – all the stronger as its prescriptions became synonymous with economic common sense. But it was only with the collapse of the Soviet Union and Eastern bloc alternatives that globalisation became fully established as the new map of the world.

Henceforth globalisation, and its core policies such as deregulation, took on a 'natural' quality as the right ordering of economics. To disclaim this proposition was like denying that the sun would rise tomorrow. But for ideas to achieve this status, to define a map of the world in this hegemonic fashion, is an aspect of power. In retrospect, the new post-Cold War order was characterised by this soft projection of US power – and this took place alongside military adventures in the Middle East associated with control of oil reserves – in a sustained policy push to finalise the unfinished business of the neo-liberal project started after the Second World War.

Since its formation in 1947, negotiations within the framework of the General Agreement on Tariffs and Trade (GATT) have successfully reduced many protectionist tariff barriers with beneficial effects for international trade, largely but not exclusively for the industrialised world. The price of foreign imported goods has been progressively reduced by removing frontier charges. The fast developing South East Asian countries greatly benefited, showing rapid growth as they exported on the back of their domestic markets. Nonetheless, even during the 1980s, the USA retained dominance over Japan and potential South East Asian competitors – but not over the European Union – in key sectors, notably industrialised agriculture, protected by subsidies, and in financial services, protected by the US Treasury and the IMF. The promotion of its superiority in so-called Trade Related Aspects of Intellectual Property Rights (TRIPS), universalising patenting rights over key forms of information with profitable potential – soon to include the human genome as well as patenting of 'transgenic' plant varieties and seeds – was also on the agenda.

So the USA had a number of goals when the Uruguay Round of the GATT opened in the 1980s: to force open world markets for its financial services sector and its agricultural produce (highly subsidised through support payments to farmers of one kind or another). There was also a push on creating a globalised patent system to exploit new plants and seeds, and pressure to maximise US advantage in software, pharmaceuticals, entertainment and chemicals. None of this was plausibly in the interests of the poor of the developing world. Financial liberalisation potentially jeopardised livelihoods in South East Asia, as governments lost control of a key sector of the economy, and the middle classes were tempted into investing in US-induced bubbles. Agricultural liberalisation threatened hopes of creating self-sustainable agriculture – the poor feeding themselves. As for patents, of the 90,948 applications filed under the current Patent Co-operation Treaty by the World Intellectual Property Organisation (WIPO) in 2001, only 5.2% came from developing countries, and most of these came from China, India, Korea and Mexico.[19]

By the time the Round was concluded in 1993, US agricultural objectives were more or less successfully achieved. The USA was greatly aided in promoting an agricultural agreement by using a multilateral approach through the 15-strong Cairns Group made up of the major grain-exporting countries. The Agreement on Agriculture specified that the developed countries had to open up the equivalent of 5% of their domestic production to imported agricultural produce (4% for the developing countries), and phased in cuts in subsidies, 36% over six years for developed countries, and 24% over ten years for developing countries. The 48 least developed countries were exempt from these cuts. But in the event the subsidies paid to the developed world's agricultural sector doubled from 1995 to 1998; rich governments found it politically expedient to pay for their agriculture. An American farmer will be getting $20,000 annually in subsidies from the 2002 US Farm Bill support, while his Mexican counterpart a few miles down the road gets $800 from his government if he is lucky. No 'level playing field' here.[20]

A striking contemporary example of this stark absence of a 'level playing field' is Africa's difficulty in marketing cotton. African cotton production today makes up 16% of world production. Not only does cotton production employ ten million Africans, but it has been one of the few means of stimulating 'linkage' to new industrial development open to African nations. Factory production of cooking oil, animal feeds and soap from cottonseed arose from an agricultural base in the desert-edge nations around the Sahara. But Africa has been and is facing intense competition from cotton producers around the world who, to a remarkable degree, are directly subsidised for the cotton that they produce.

Farmers producing cotton in the USA and Europe during 2001 received government subsidies of 1.21 Euros and 1.49 Euros respectively per kilo of cotton. The level of subsidy was 25% and 50% *more than the sale price of a kilo of cotton*, which traded at around 0.95 Euros. So US and European farmers have – and have had – a spectacular advantage in the market. Not surprisingly what Africa has been able to earn from the price of its cotton on the world market has dropped threefold in real terms over the last thirty years as the continent faced the additional problem of synthetic fibres flooding the market and reducing demand.[21]

It might have been expected that after the advent of the WTO, with its principle of the level playing field, subsidies for cotton would have begun dropping in line with decreases in direct subsidies to food crops. But not so: 50% of world production received direct subsidies in 1998; subsidies were given on 73% of production in 2001. Today some $360 billion is spent on *subsidies* to agricultural producers in the richer North compared to a grand total of $54 billion in *aid* given to the South, much of it tied to production in the North. At the G8 in Evian in 2003 the US refused to budge on its outrageous payment of £1.8 billion per annum in hidden subsidies to its 25,000 cotton farmers. Despite this, African cotton as shown by its market share has struggled to remain competitive – at the expense of the producer. But for how much longer?[22]

So there is a strong element of hypocrisy in the avowed commitment to Africa's development of the USA and European Union. Their trade policies have slowly but surely blocked promising avenues for rural development. 'Development' must mean rectifying this damage. But the planned rate of removal of tariffs on key Third World exports, agriculture, textiles and footwear, is much slower than that on the industrially produced goods of the OECD. Whether it is citrus fruits, aluminium or steel, when push comes to shove, neo-liberalism gives way to protective tariffs designed to consolidate votes in key sections of the electorates of the North. That these decisions fly in the face of proclaimed economic orthodoxy is glossed over. The USA has national 'unfair trade' laws but, in the words of Joseph Stiglitz, a past chief economist to the World Bank who should know, 'they exist solely to protect American industries adversely affected by imports'.[23]

The World Bank has calculated that Africa would earn 14% more annually, the equivalent of $2.5 billion of lost revenue, if all – including hidden – forms of protection were removed by the USA, Japan and the European Union. The short-term interest of a few national producers in the developed world, mainly those whose votes are deemed critical in elections, continue to be placed above those of populations on the borderline of starvation. The net result is that Africa with 10% of the world's population benefits from barely 2% of the world's trade and investment.[24]

Broad agreements on Trade in Services (GATS) and TRIPS were also put in place during the Uruguay Round, the former fought for by the European Union against resistance from the developing countries. The theory behind GATS was, again, that of 'comparative advantage', that the system should encourage the most efficient providers and producers for the good of all. So incoming international companies should be given a virtually free hand with no special treatment by government for domestic entrepreneurs. Nor could there be any insistence by government, for example, on the use of local material, local food or local labour in new internationally owned hotels to maximise beneficial linkages arising from the tourist trade. Theoretically, all things being equal, out of this raw competition would come new advantageous forms of economic activity in the developing world. 'Uncompetitive' enterprises would wither away in a process of creative destruction. But all things were anything but equal.

The USA also got much of what it wanted on the TRIPS front, but was constrained by the developing countries' insistence on abiding by the 1993 UN Convention on Biological Diversity and the International Undertaking on Plant Genetic Resources. In consequence existing life forms, plants and animals, could not be legally patented. But the big corporations' right to patent the genetic processes involved in creating new transgenic, 'GM', varieties and seeds, was recognised as an intellectual property right in the agreement. Most important, the forty odd countries that did not provide patent protection for pharmaceutical products and processes were obliged to get into line. The further elaboration of the Agreement on Trade-Related Aspects of Intellectual Property Rights, particularly its impact on the provision of public health by member states, had to await the formation of the WTO.

The subsequent formation of the World Trade Organisation (WTO) from the GATT on 1 January 1995, created a new world body, some half century after it had first been envisioned by Bretton Woods. It had authority to exercise an international judicial function through the recommendations of its Dispute Settlement and Appellate Boards and was capable of enforcing the compliance of offending states by authorising retaliatory economic action. In addition it offered some machinery for the developing world to get its views formally heard. George Soros has described the WTO as 'in many ways the most advanced and fully developed of our international institutions'. His description indicates how potential global institutions, as measured by contemporary funding, are ranked; the WTO based in Geneva started out with only 450 staff and an annual budget of $83 million, less than several large charities.[25]

Nor did the WTO break the mould of the politicised pro-rich world bodies. As Soros freely admits, 'the critics are right in claiming that the WTO is biased in favour of the rich countries and multinational corporations' even though its procedures were *intended* to enforce a level playing field for trading nations.[26] The bias towards the powerful, though, was strongest outside its doors. The USA exerted pressure on member states to submit to what amounted to 'TRIPS-Plus', an approach to the agreement that required accelerated implementation with no recourse to its flexible provisions for the developing nations. In other words what the USA would have liked to have imposed multilaterally, but could not, it was going to impose unilaterally. States found themselves suffering economic sanctions and loss of preferential access to US markets if they did not comply with TRIPS-Plus.

One of the first tasks mooted for the WTO was to push forward agreement on Trade Related Investment Measures (TRIMS) by preparing a Multilateral Agreement on Investment (MAI). This was designed to give the vast multinational corporations 'no worse' treatment from government – in other words they were open to negotiate out of strength for better treatment – than smaller national companies. It was to be open season for the financial services sector. But the opportunity for concerted developing country input to the agreement, however modest, dictated that negotiations take place outside the WTO in the rich countries' club of the OECD (Organisation for Economic Co-operation and Development). In this way, the developing world would be obliged to sign up to a document about which they had not been consulted, or face the consequences – a probable blight on foreign investment to their countries.

The MAI negotiations finally collapsed from a combination of pressures, most notably entrenched objections from France. Opposition from the NGOs had been persistent and French NGOs may have been instrumental in strengthening their government's resolve on the issue. What did go forward in the WTO was a Financial

Services Agreement, but this was also negotiated into the buffers by an overbearing USA. This time Malaysia refused to be rolled over and led a brave coalition of the unwilling, resisting opening their markets on US terms to US financial institutions.

US pressure for 'liberalisation', the opening up of financial services markets, was sustained throughout the 1990s through a range of institutions, and with broad support from the European Union, particularly the United Kingdom. At the Asia-Europe Heads of State meeting in 1997 in London, I listened with growing amazement to encomia on neo-liberal doctrine issuing from the platform. The Asian crisis was upon them; 13 million Asians were in the process of losing their jobs. Thailand was to suffer a 10.8% drop in GDP in 1998 whilst in South Korea urban poverty soared. The succession of prime ministers and heads of state singing the praises of neo-liberal policies was reminiscent of the speeches of Politburo members who had to thank Comrade Stalin if they were to get home safely.

The South East Asian crisis was being attributed to 'crony capitalism' at the time. But how, Joseph Stiglitz wondered, 'if these countries' institutions were so rotten, had they done so well for so long?'.[27] Indeed they had been seen as models of impressive economic growth. The Asian way to capitalism had been admired and studied. The answer to Stiglitz's rhetorical question was, of course, that the crisis had been created by too rapid a process of liberalisation, massive flows of footloose and short-term foreign capital that, after fuelling a property boom, was precipitately withdrawn. And currency speculation had not been checked by a massive $98 billion bailout for the region. Moreover, the situation was made far worse by the IMF's insistence on its traditional package of high-interest rates and fiscal austerity – as if the South East Asian economies were as weak as those of the Latin American states in the 1980s, and as if the problem lay with *governments'* failure to pay their debts rather than lending and borrowing banks.

Meanwhile the USA wielded its 18% weighted voting power in the International Monetary Fund (IMF), and its links with top officials, to promote its policies. Countries with voting records in the General Assembly deemed insufficiently pro-USA could face insuperable difficulties in getting loans. As if this was not enough, as the South East Asian economies collapsed, the US Treasury was also pressing to get the IMF's Articles of Association changed. This was to give the body greater power to oblige member countries to liberalise their current accounts, and let foreign money in and out. Elsewhere, the pressure was exerted in bilateral relations with every effort made to prise open Asian markets. Irrespective of your specific economic ills, the neo-liberal prescription would be good for you, went the refrain . . . and, anyway, you had no choice. The success of this economic strategy may be measured in the South East Asian led contagion of 1997 to 1999 and the flight from the dollar after the US stock market collapse of 2002.

BANKERS BEHAVING BADLY

The two key inter-state players determining the direction of globalisation are the International Monetary Fund (IMF) and the World Bank (WB), the offspring of Bretton Woods. While there is evidence that coalitions of NGOs can influence the international financial institutions – the Jubilee campaign did influence the leadership of the World Bank – it is essentially member nation-state representatives of these bodies who have the power to bring about change, the most important being, of course, the USA. Throughout the critical period of the 1980s and 1990s, these appointed representatives negotiated on key issues beyond public scrutiny and appeared, from what little is known of their decision-making processes, to represent financial or trade interests. Moreover, the internal dynamics of each institution, and its external relations to key US departments of state, were laws unto themselves.

Together with the regional banks, the World Bank showed more capacity for learning from experience, more interest in transparency, and was less rigidly doctrinaire in policy prescription than the IMF. But until the late 1990s this was not saying much. The World Bank has been the major multilateral development source for lending to governments, particularly project lending (microeconomic measures), involving a large 'hands-on' staff. It first met the long-term capital needs of a war-shattered Europe before focusing on global development. When it came to policing economies, it played NYPD to the Fund's FBI.

The sights of the smaller IMF were more narrowly focussed on managing balance of payments crises by shorter-term capital provision and bridging loans to restore overall macroeconomic balance. It bailed out governments that had got into debt – at a price. The original vision of both institutions owed much to Maynard Keynes: the stimulation of domestic and global demand in economic downturns, through making capital available for expansionary policies, was initially viewed as a central part of their role. The methodology of both changed and tended to converge on similar neo-liberal economic prescriptions in the last quarter century.

The 1980s policy shift to 'market fundamentalism' saw the heritage of the more Keynesian World Bank President, Robert McNamara, give way before the ideas of a free marketeer, William Clausen. Into the role of chief economist came a trade expert, Ann Krueger, who shared his views. She had a leery view of debtor governments' economic interventions: they served the interests of national elites who benefited from protectionist measures. Failed development came from too much government involvement in too little market. At the same time the IMF increasingly came under the influence of the US Treasury and began to reflect the political priorities of the US government. Keynes' emphasis on governments' role in job creation and in rectifying market 'failures' faded away. Hyper-inflation, bureaucratic budgets out of control, corrupt elites using government intervention for personal enrichment, these were the enemy. Not surprisingly it was the mess in the 'backyard', the political economy of their southern neighbour, Mexico, and of Latin America as a whole, that informed thinking – a cautionary tale indeed.[28]

During the 1980s the World Bank was obliged to react to debt crises. They surfaced threateningly with the Mexican *peso* crisis in 1982. The growing role of commercial banks in Third World debt, and the onset of global economic problems in 1979 to 1980, were ominous signs. As a result the Bank was pushed into a major interest in macroeconomic policy, the IMF's bailiwick. The dominant theory of development in the next decade therefore hinged on financial stability, meaning in practice the stability of the financial sector. The jobs of OECD workers in the finance sector, not the jobs of the poor in the developing world, came first. This might be disguised by talk of 'painful medicine', with jam not tomorrow but some time in the future, but, as Keynes, rightly observed 'in the long term we are all dead'. The developing world was condemned to a decade of development disaster.

The Bank's 1981 *Agenda for Action* spoke of 'conditionality'. This made financial support conditional on adopting a package of measures that found their rationale in neo-liberal orthodoxy. The agenda was designed to reduce state intervention, improve public sector management and cull slothful overblown bureaucracies, so restoring the capacity of governments to service their debts. Big loans to government required the approval of the IMF. This provided the gold standard of creditworthiness, entailed strict conditions, and opened other doors to credit.

A fundamentalist economic 'medicine' was prescribed for all circumstances in a variety of mixes. The World Bank ingredients were: a focus on agriculture by improving support, marketing and revision of agricultural pricing; improving efficiency of the public sector particularly financial performance; reforming the tax system; removing import quotas; and increasing export incentives. Such a package had to be agreed to get a loan, and seen to be honoured to keep it running. This set of conditions became universally known as structural adjustment. Its content was a set of measures presented as the formula for generating sustainable growth.

The shaky theoretical background to structural adjustment was the core diagnosis that the success of development hinged on a polarity between state versus market. The least developed nations were in a parlous condition because of state capitalism, interventionism and bureaucracy. They needed more control from the market and less from the state, more specifically they needed a programme of reduced state intervention – privatisation – coupled with higher interest rates and export-led recovery.[29]

Much of this had a superficial plausibility. My many visits to the labyrinthine Nigerian bureaucracy in the 1970s, for example, were instructive. On a good day, officials resplendent in pastel shades could be caught turning the pages of the Nigerian Press to find who was up and who was down, much as the *Racing Times* would be studied for form. Ceiling fans whirred. Languid glances. The gaze of a minor guardian of the dusty files would settle on you with a mixture of amusement and disdain. On a bad day, the trick was to catch the man needed 'on seat'. The advanced trick, far more complex and requiring refinements of etiquette and polite banter, was to get him to retrieve your file. Then the game began. Government in Africa often seemed to me like a cruel Byzantine joke played on the masses as their reward for escaping colonialism. The international financial institutions were half right, but they had a dangerously partial explanation of the problem.

Though the IMF were true believers in neo-liberal fundamentalism, and the World Bank less so, and indeed increasingly more revisionist in their approach, there was a clear policy consensus. The 'Washington Consensus' articulated orthodoxy through a variety of international policy interventions. Outside of the US Treasury, the World Bank and IMF supplied the most persuasive missionaries. The more mundane background to these offers that you refused at your peril was that they offered the best chance of western creditor banks getting most of their money back from heavily indebted countries on the verge of default. The US Treasury saw them encapsulating USA's interests.

An approach to the international financial institutions for a loan was a critical moment for governments, the time for at least a temporary willingness to take external advice. And advice in the form of conditionality demands, and additional indoctrination, was willingly given. The WB and IMF priesthood became the missionary teaching orders of neo-liberalism, flying round the world, spreading the ideology, visiting their adherents in ministries of finance and Treasuries, and, sometimes, mediating and moderating the worst excesses of market fundamentalism to the faithful. Yet it amounted to an important extent to 'conversion under duress', creating resentment and backsliding.

This religious analogy is not just a literary device. A quasi-religion, economics lies somewhere between dogmatics and science in its willingness to change course when disproved by empirical evidence. The evidence and pressures have to build up overwhelmingly for change to occur. Then a change in paradigm can be sudden.

Like religious dogmas the IMF's precise policy prescriptions appear to have been dispensed as if political and social questions were an irrelevant externality. The one thing their advice was not was contextual. In 2002, in Malawi, a country noted for droughts and poor governance, the IMF recommended the selling of its grain reserves to repay a loan to a South African bank; all 167,000 metric tonnes were sold. By April, corruption around the sale was rampant and, by October, hundreds of villagers were eating roots and starving. Rwanda on the eve of the worst genocide since the Holocaust embarked on a prescribed structural adjustment programme that rapidly increased short-term poverty and youth unemployment. So, in comparison, how should we rate a religious refusal to allow a vital blood transfusion, or a widow following her husband to a funeral pyre? Mildly damaging perhaps?

By 1994, as the World Bank and IMF marked the fiftieth anniversary of their founding at Bretton Woods, there was not a lot to celebrate. They were under attack from both the Right – not neo-liberal enough – and the Left – too neo-liberal. Moreover, the weight of evidence was shifting from equivocal to negative as far as the impact of structural adjustment on long-term development was concerned. For Latin America and Africa, the 1980s had seen a sharp decline in average incomes. For Africa a one-third increase in incomes between 1960 and 1980 had turned into a one-quarter decline in the following two decades marked by liberalisation. Structural adjustment programmes and attempts to stabilise economies had produced 'disappointing results' or 'a lost decade of development' according to perspective.

As the development economist Frances Stewart pointed out in an UNCTAD paper, the conditions required for liberalisation to succeed were simply ignored. 'Trade liberalisation may increase labour-intensive exports in countries with abundant labour, but only if infrastructure is adequate and the labour has at least minimal education.'[30] That ruled out nearly all the least developed countries. The impact of the Uruguay Round of the GATT on Africa was calculated to be a net 2% decline in income. The official response to evidence that things were going wrong, rolled out in the early 1990s, was more time for the medicine to work, plus additional ingredients. The 'add-ons' amounted to investment in public goods: infrastructure, human capital – for example education and training and with a focus on health – with poverty reduction as a growing theme of Bank projects. Acknowledgement that the theoretical framework itself might be inherently defective was taboo.

It was the IMF's handling of the transition in Russia that finally undermined market fundamentalism. Applying textbook economics, in a shock liberalisation and privatisation, without any sense that the absence of the institutions required for market economics to work might have severe consequences, the advisers presided over the most precipitate collapse of a major political economy since the Bolshevik Revolution. Industrial output from the fall of the Berlin Wall until 1997 declined by 41%, and, by the end of the century, GDP had dropped by a staggering 54%. In human terms almost a quarter of the population descended into poverty. But the rich oligarchy got spectacularly richer, recycling the bail-out package of IMF dollars into their foreign bank accounts. In the words of Yeltsin adviser, Anatoly Chubais: 'we conned them (the USA) out of $20 billion'. That must have hurt – though the amount was small compared to the recent US Savings and Loans scandal in the USA that cost the government $200 billion in the subsequent bail-out.[31]

As the IMF was enriching a handful of crooks in Moscow, the consequences of their prescriptions in Asia were coming home to roost in the Asian crisis. Notwithstanding, a similar set of revised but damaging policy prescriptions was wheeled out to deal with the Asian meltdown and duly aggravated the crisis for a number of Asian countries. Finally, and only after it was clear that countries such as Malaysia and China, which had ignored their prescriptions, were suffering a far less severe downturn, some IMF backtracking occurred.

THE POST-WASHINGTON TRANSITION

In 1998, admissions were at last made that they had been getting some things wrong, that there had been policy mistakes. As the World Bank variant of diluted neo-liberalism was reaching the end of its theoretical tether, its chief economist and Senior Vice President, Joe Stiglitz, delivered a speech suggesting a way out. 'Trying to get government focused on the fundamentals – economic policies, basic education, health, roads, law and order, environmental protection – is a vital step,' he declared. But this bundle of socio-economic and environmental goods had never been the 'fundamentals' of the fundamentalists. The game was up. Stiglitz was advocating a major shift.[32]

A past chairman of the US Council of Economic Advisers, Stiglitz's speech signalled a U-turn. It was as if Alan Greenspan of the Federal Reserve had said that he was giving up trying to control inflation. Yet

Stiglitz remained within a market versus state analysis and swept aside criticism of the underlying model. He attributed the failure of structural adjustment to an inadequate understanding of the role of 'information' in 'market imperfections', thereby opening the way for a more muscular state to rectify them ... with suitable measures directed by the World Bank. Thus carefully swaddled in abstract economic theory, was the 'post-Washington consensus' born. A more popular and Keynesian version of this new consensus was presented in *Globalisation and its Discontents*, published by Stiglitz four years later.

Probably under pressure from Japan, which saw no reason to fund policies that amounted to a repudiation of methods that had guided its economic success in the 1980s, the pendulum had swung back towards a strong, or at least a stronger, state. For his pains, Stiglitz resigned from his job – though he got a Nobel Prize – and wrote his discontented indictment of the IMF's record. But his salvage recommendations were essentially followed. 'Good governance', antidote to 'market imperfections', became the buzzword of policy-makers, hiding the theoretical U-turn. The new prescription with its unprecedented potential for political intervention by the Bank was implemented. Whether or not the state versus market polarity remains a helpful one is a moot point. Though it was roundly declared 'left behind' by all in authority, it remains operationally highly significant.[33]

As the World Bank began to part company with the IMF, selling this new consensus, and level of intervention, to Third World governments became essential. There was now an emphasis on process and procedures. In 1999 the World Bank set out to write Poverty Reduction Strategy Papers for countries and solicited inputs and consultation on their final form from governments and organis-ations in civil society. Policy ownership was now the name of the game. As the Holy Qu'ran taught that there should be 'no coercion in religion', so the Bank proclaimed that there should be 'no coercion in economics'. In parenthesis this change of tack to the 'soft cop' approach to shaping the world might be set alongside the new US policy of pre-emptive military intervention against forms of 'bad governance' that were allegedly threatening the USA.

'Policy ownership' for the cynics meant seeking to create the appearance of states doing what the Bank wanted willingly and cooperatively. Or, more charitably, the result of taking the Bank's new insight seriously meant that participation by organisations of the poor in poverty reduction put pressure on government to buy into pro-poor policies. Consultation undoubtedly provided an opportunity for 'empowerment', assuming local NGOs existed and could get together and respond in time – and some did – and assuming government was willing to countenance NGO involvement. In some countries – Yemen would be an example – there was little answering to the name 'civil society', except some university intellectuals and Muslim student associations, able to offer a cogent critique. But even when a well-developed NGO sector existed, the information gap between the Bank and groups in civil society was, of course, huge.[34]

The emphasis on consultation was nonetheless new and important. It may have resulted in little substantive input to the Poverty Reduction Strategy Papers, but it revealed to NGOs how far they had to go in influencing policy debates in the developing world. At least the Bank's top leadership is now fully behind the 2015 International Development Targets of halving world poverty and a new policy emphasis on poverty reduction. Evidence could be marshalled for both the cynical and the charitable assessment of the changes, but it was more than 'tweaking'.

Aside from the debt-reduction campaign of the NGOs conducted between 1996 and 2002, the international financial institutions have set most of the agenda and framework for aid and development for the last quarter century. Their achievement has been to hold their own against the isolationist political Right in the USA. The post-Washington consensus – which is, of course, no consensus at all within the USA – represents an important approach to globalisation that has been adopted with modifications by a number of European social democrat governments. It is, of course, flawed. It avoids completely any in-depth critique of the international financial architecture, whose weakness threatens development targets, and has a very narrow cultural account of what equals 'economic, social and political progress'. It is still a long way from a concept of integral human development.

Moreover, on a global rather than national or regional scale it relies for the provision of public goods – one of the main targets of aid – on a UN system that is under-funded, often endowed with poor leadership, and with negligible US support. Indeed for many of the ultra-nationalists in the USA, including the powerful cabal around President Bush, the UN appears as an impediment to the projection of US power. So the political economy of globalisation suffers from the grave asymmetry of global economic power unconstrained by global political order. The problem of global governance is thus the most critical one confronting contemporary market-based growth of the global economy.

This chapter has attempted to chart the origins and growth of our global political economy and to digest the contentious and complex role of the USA, international financial institutions and multi-nationals as its dominant political actors. It has no less been the story of the Prometheus unbound of finance capital and flows. It would, however, be misleading to reduce the process of globalisation to the economic. There is more to it than that. Economics and governance are both aspects of culture, and it is to the wider question of future cultural change that the next chapter turns.

CHAPTER 5

CHANGING SPACES

Who in the fifteenth century would have guessed that the printing press was going to transform European culture? How many people in St Petersburg in 1917 would have predicted what was in store for them during the next seventy years? From the midst of rapid change, it is never easy to gauge the magnitude of what is going on or what it means. The new political economy of globalisation seems to suggest change of comparable magnitude, perhaps even greater. Our economics, how we make a living, is undergoing a sea change. On its tide are carried extraordinary advances in genetic engineering, biotechnology and communications, which may lead us to re-interpret what it means to be human.

So where is all this heading? What does it mean for us? One way to seek an answer is to extrapolate from the processes we observe today, in an attempt to generate a predictive theory of social change. For the moral significance of globalisation cannot be comprehensively described in an ethics of economic change. There are social and cultural questions that must be explored if we are to get any indication whether our contemporary moral language and past experience will suffice in the future.

Changes in economies are measured quantitatively even though economists aspire to grand theories. And analysis of the political economy of globalisation demands accurate statistics. For most people equations and econometric models provide a less meaningful picture of a changing world than the qualitative social and cultural transformations that accompany or follow in the wake of changes in the political economy. The recent figures are certainly prodigious: US$ 350 trillion in the form of casino-chip packages of 'derivatives' were traded in the electronic circuits of cyberspace in 1997 alone. But are contemporary social and cultural changes equally great? And, if the answer is no, is it just a matter of time before they begin to signify a profound change in society?

'Trouble up at mill' is less the worry today. It is losses in the money markets, trouble in the City of London, that spells disaster, and for millions. This is because capital is mainly invested and accumulated in the sphere of circulation. The value of most circulating capital is realised in the virtual reality of cyberspace. Those symbols on the screen may look merely like little electronic blobs but when they change, people and countries get richer or poorer in the blink of an eye. The stock exchange and the floors of capital-trading rooms have become the theatres of wealth creation. This pre-eminence of finance capital in the process of globalisation is the defining feature of the nascent global economy. Power lies in mastering these flows.

This extraordinary sea change in the global economic system does not provide the key to globalisation in the sense of a simple explanatory blueprint from which all else follows. The shape of society and culture cannot be constructed as a visible superstructure arising from a hidden economic infrastructure of financial flows. Such a simple chain of causality, once dear to vulgar forms of Marxism, entirely misplaces the importance and complexity of human consciousness and agency. We make our own history. It is not simply made for us by machines and delineated by economic models. More important, attributing world transformations to a single cause, economic change, neglects the complexity of interactions. These take place most notably in two spheres: between our use of technology and the perennial restructuring of business enterprises in response to shocks; the shape of contemporary social interactions and the generation, or erosion, of cultural values that derive from changing human experience. 'Globalisation' encompasses the outcomes of all these multiple interactions.[1]

Moreover, any worthwhile account of where we are heading requires fine judgements on just how nascent is the nascent global economy. 'What has really changed?' is the question. 'Not the kind of activities that humankind is engaged in, but its technological ability to use as a direct productive force what distinguishes our species as a biological oddity: its superior ability to process symbols' is the conclusion of the leading theoretician and analyst of contemporary socio-economic change, Manuel Castells.[2] This is the consequence of the productive power of the new information and communications technology. Waves of new product lines, mobile phones, CD-ROMs, DVDs, each processing their digitised signals, have appeared in fast succession. People discard old means of communication and buy the new to do what they had always done, communicate with each other, listen to music and be entertained. These obvious continuities persist.

So how different from our world today was the social and cultural world of 1971, when the microprocessor was invented and the core infrastructure of the information revolution began to be laid down? Some degree of structural transformation has undeniably occurred, a reshaping of work and society, but in ways that are hard to quantify. The bigger question has to be posed: to what extent have recent extraordinary advances in microelectronics, software – and genetic engineering – and their immediate and long-term consequences, pushed us into a new historic epoch, the beginnings of a new society? This is what Castells sets out to examine.

His answer is that the birth of a new society, a change in epochs, arises when structural transformation may be observed in the relationships of *all* of the following: production, power and experience.[3] Few would disagree that the industrial revolution led to such a transformation in Europe, that the distinction between 'industrial' and 'agricultural' worlds delineates two broad and pervasive check-lists of differences that add up to something qualitative and important. There is general agreement that how people earned their living, experienced it and organised society changed dramatically.

So Castells offers his own account of the new 'information economy' and its world. The key feature of its social morphology, literally the shape of things to come, is the dominance of complex networks. The growth of a 'network society' sums up the social relationships of a dominant new mode of production based on control of information. This change is spearheaded by the network structure of multinational corporations (MNCs), crossing national boundaries or barriers, with complex links to subsidiary supplier companies and components manufacturers, and, later, by international non-governmental organisations (INGOs). States do not lose their importance, but their importance is modified.[4] To retain their power they have to tap into the network to capture and distribute – or restructure and redistribute – flows of information and wealth.

According to his argument, we have passed, or are passing today, from industrial to information society. Superimposed on the old maps made up of nation-states we need to superimpose a new network map. The space that increasingly matters in this mode of production is not a local workplace but a medium of flows, most notably the flow of different forms of exchange value, electronic money, what sometimes seems like an infinite regress of symbols denoting symbols. When a Korean company closed its factory in a Welsh Valley in 1998, hundreds suffered, but when the stock exchange crashed in 2001, millions paid the price, particularly the poor and elderly whose pensions were hit. And, of course, the closure of the Korean company was one of several consequences of the tidal flow of capital withdrawn from Korea by investors and currency speculators – each changing little symbols in cyberspace to influence the market.[5]

A working definition of crude power is the ability, by whatever means, to enforce behaviour. Today economic power lies in the control of capital flows. Cultural, 'soft', power of which it is a part has the wider remit: control of 'the network of information, exchange and symbol manipulation which relate social actors, institutions and cultural movements through icons, spokespersons, and intellectual amplifiers', or, more simply control of 'life's interpretative keys'.[6] This includes the obvious economic dimension of controlling, or influencing, the world of advertising and the mass media, the manipulation of desire.

An imperative for the exercise of political power, control of key TV channels, played an important part in getting Silvio Berlusconi elected in Italy. Lula had to get Brazilian stations on side to reach the Presidency. Clinton and Blair perfected the techniques of 'instant rebuttal' with sophisticated Press teams. Such cultural forms of soft power are routinely encountered, in pure form, in the promotion, channelling and 'framing' of fears and hopes by political elites and governments, particularly in relation to selected internal and external 'enemies' – and always have been. And soft power, of course, may potentially be used against the state.

Perhaps one of the best recent illustrations lies in the realm of counter-force wielded against the state. Sub-Commandante Marcos led an armed Zapatista revolution in Chiapas against the Mexican government in the mid-1990s but used information and electronic communication from a jungle base to force spectacular concessions with minimal use of military force. Cartoons and the Zapatistas' charming 'cyber-panache' were as important a weapon against the Mexican government as guns. In a different way, the vast proliferation of modern advertising and the rise of the 'logo' companies, such as McDonalds, Walt Disney and Nike, have created new commercial battalions engaged in 'symbol wars'. They exert prodigious power – and use a great deal of money – to manipulate the potent world of cultural codes and symbols to change human experience in favour of their lines of goods.[7]

Our human experience is always culturally coded, so to talk of changes in experience is to talk also of changes in culture. European missionary visions of the Blessed Virgin, pasty white, dressed in blue, with roses on her toes reflected the idiom of a certain period of Italianate art. Will pious African Catholics see the same figure in a baobab tree, or will the Blessed Virgin be black? That will depend on the strength and retention of an older style of European mission culture. One recent sighting from Rwanda split the difference; Our Lady was brown – and used to legitimate the corrupt and racist government of President Juvenal Habyarimana. There is no such thing as the experience of 'uncoded' reality; our purchase on reality is both neurologically and culturally mediated. So control of cultural codes, how we interpret our world, is an important terrain of ethical and political struggle, where culture meets commerce. This is not news to the vast media conglomerates Times–Warner and News International. The rise of the Internet and new mixed media have introduced powerful new weapons onto this terrain. That is why authoritarian regimes are working hard to control access to them.

Once 'on-line' a simple touch on a keyboard is all that is required to jump from one world, one message, to another. 'The choice of various messages under the same communication mode, with easy switching from one to the other, reduces the mental distance between various sources of cognitive and sensorial involvement,' Castells asserts. He believes this matters because Broadband transmission and the Internet, for example, permit 'a random mixture of various realms of coded experience and meanings resulting in a blurring of codes'.[8]

This sounds plausible. The richness and diversity of human experience is captured in compressed time and space, no longer embedded in a local social and political context, historical sequence or human sensibility. So it might be that we are in danger of losing our capacity for distinguishing ethical and political codes from a plethora of trivial choices. It may be this is why we are finding it so hard to build political community and have difficulties taking history seriously. Past, present and future become co-terminous in the 'now' of information flows.

In short, Castells' proposition is this, and it cannot be dismissed out of hand even though it has the smack of science fiction: cyber-space, a universal realm of communication, opens up a radically new chapter for humanity with some serious dangers. It is one of the Janus faces of globalisation. Virtuality, the way things are in cyber-space, may become for power, production and experience – perhaps already is – the dominant space and time, the one that matters most and most powerfully defines what happens, who gets rich, who gets poor, whether we destroy our planet. And, most important, this new world of virtuality will erode our capacity for rootedness in places and in living traditions, for commitment and attachment, taking root and touching ground, for visualising future projects.

Human life and identity may begin to have two principal dimensions: we will live in clock time, in a particular place and country, alongside living in a new 'timeless time' in a new 'space of flows' through information technology. To be or not to be present in the new space and new time will then be the future touchstone of inclusion and exclusion. Everywhere else becomes defined as 'periphery'. People living only in the old time and in old – local – places will become marginal and powerless. Lacking technology they will lack vital knowledge, refused credit they will not be engaged in production for the market; they will be induced to want what they can never have, and they will experience radical insecurity. The new and the old will both have a geographical manifestation: those with access to cyberspace, the new artisans and masters of financial flows and cultural codes, will cluster in cities and information technology rich nodes or centres linked in an information network. This is his future map of the world.[9]

THE NETWORK MAP

'Well, up to a point Lord Copper.' This is stimulating futurology. And we need a usable sociological vision that is more sophisticated than glib references to 'the global village'. But the difficulty with this vision lies in taking trends and intimations of where structural transformations are leading to their limits. And history repeatedly refuses to move in straight lines when it moves towards limits. There was nothing straight about the line from the Enlightenment to Auschwitz. Castells delineates the contours of a possible future, but he is parsimonious about supporting it with compelling empirical evidence.[10]

Power still manifestly lies in military force as the final arbiter of political differences. True, for successful projection of power, the propaganda war and fight for moral legitimacy grows in importance in democracies, and the communications revolution is obviously a substantive new factor in this cultural struggle. But micro-electronic technology is no less important in the development of 'smart' weapons that allow 'precision' bombing. This gives rise to spurious but telling claims about the legitimacy of wars conducted by the owners of such weaponry: fewer civilians allegedly get killed. Moreover, the provision of real-time information flows to frontline troops is likely to revolutionise command-and-control structures, and thus the conduct of future warfare. Of course the capacity to build up high-technology military force depends on accumulated past wealth and expertise generated by, amongst other factors, command of the informational economy. But military power is itself significantly modified by communications technology.

Castells' assumption is that cyberspace, the 'space of flows', inevitably marginalizes other spaces or localities, and will eventually overwhelm their social significance. A hard empirical look at contemporary social adaptations to the communications revolution does not bear this out. Human relationships give to space form, function and social meaning. But this is no less true of the virtual domains and web sites in cyberspace than of the real space of altars, housing estates, manned spacecraft, African villages or the Twin Towers. Cyberspace is more clearly the domain of the ephemeral. It is obviously the realm of the non-contiguous.

And yet what about the spatial contiguity of three airliners to buildings in New York and Washington – with their victims and suicide bombers? These were buildings of great symbolic significance, and the real-time of these terrorist events and their aftermath, the stark locality and ticking clock of Ground Zero, are palpably not a marginal form of space and time. True, the impact of these events in real time and space is immeasurably augmented by being repeatedly played in the mass media out of clock time. But this particular locality, and its ephemeral event, is about as powerful and global as it gets. And, yes, soap operas can also have a remarkable degree of impact on public behaviour, and they go on being played on the next channel alongside repeats of the Towers coming down. But are the codes of each of these various messages 'blurred' by those who receive and interpret the images? No, people get the message all right. Ask the Taliban.

Whether it is interaction between religious fundamentalists across the world via web sites, or women prostituting their bodies with clients in 'virtual brothels', 'blurring' of codes is not the most notable feature of 'time sharing social practices' in cyberspace. Instead an extension, and sometimes mobilisation, of already existing subcultures can occur. At least it can occur in those able to retrieve and enhance the meaning of their particular cultural codes, structures, boundaries.

'Instant' round-the-clock time of financial flows is certainly a new kind of time, and one redolent of a power to structure reality, but a time that is set alongside, and not yet obviously overpowering, the clock time in which pubs and bars open and shut, the religious time of Easter and Ramadan, or the biological duration of a human pregnancy.

Of course communication is disembodied in cyberspace, and that may matter. But seeing the 'loss of the body' in the social relationships of new forms of communication as portentous is exaggerated. True, this may be different from telephoning a relative in Australia. Face-to-face contact may become a tragic moment of human communication for those whose daily life is socialised and given meaning through the Internet. There is something troubling about young people spending long periods in electronic 'chat-rooms'. But the telegraph, then telephone, television, video and DVD, did not effect anything like a total societal change. E-mail, Internet, texting and pagers may perhaps be a more effective means of convening like-minded people to public spaces and commons than the telephone, but this is a matter of degree. Public demonstrations such as the Vietnam peace marches arguably had no more, no less, political impact than recent ones summoned on e-mail networks.

Each technical advance illustrated many of the potentially damaging side effects of the use of more recent communications media. Like the Internet each modified existing forms of sociability and created the opportunity to construct new forms. My happiest recollection of a TV dinner was sharing a meal with a Ghanaian family in London. We all sat in special chairs, like well-behaved brown bears, smiling expectantly, napkins at the ready, while the mother of the house circulated, ladling large portions onto our plates. Nobody stopped talking. The streets of London, supposedly beset by anomie, are clogged on Sunday afternoons with carloads of families visiting relatives. The information society has increased the importance of the private space of the home, privatising public space to some degree, and reduced the frequency, though not necessarily the importance, of both routine and special gatherings in public 'real' space. This is not a revolution.

So while the evidence is not yet convincing that changes in production, power and experience in the last thirty years yet add up to the birth of a new society or signal the advent of a new epoch, they undoubtedly amplify pre-existing social and cultural trends to an unprecedented degree. Of course, the pace of these changes is sharply geographically differentiated in a complex global patchwork. The global distribution of information technology is no less skewed than the distribution of other forms of power. There are about 170 million Internet users in North America and 3.5 million in Africa, 42% and 0.75% of the world total respectively.[11]

THE APARTHEID OF INEQUALITY

The industrial North itself, in transition to an information society, has undoubtedly been subject to new forms of social differentiation. In addition information technology and intense business competition have generated new forms of production. The fast-food industry and the growth of call centres, for example, created a new class of workers with low pay and insecure prospects, casual work and short-term contracts, as has the growth of retail outlets for branded products. But to think of the world in a North-South configuration is itself problematic. The international outreach of companies and corporations put Indian workers, for example, in direct competition with British and American in the sale of their labour in the information economy.

Perhaps the most important trend emerging from the transition is the shifting power balance between capital and labour. Contemporary globalisation is tipping the scales even more – perhaps definitively – in favour of capital against labour. Companies can move around to find the labour they want but this does not apply the other way round, with the small exception of elite, skilled labour. The social consequences in the working lives of people are already visible. Inequality has intensified both nationally and internationally, forming a network of wealth, expertise and information – all interlinked – and disconnected poverty, a patchwork of affluent nodes surrounded by black holes of marginality. However, this is not necessarily to condemn globalisation as having created a net overall *increase in poverty* worldwide.

To read some of the NGOs' campaign literature, it might be imagined that no respectable arguments exist in favour of a benign role for globalisation in poverty eradication, nor that the question whether the world was getting richer, or poorer, and why, is open to debate. But the problem is asking the right questions. Whether capital is now generating more wealth with existing labour than ever before, or whether the world is a more comfortable place for more people to live in than in previous generations is not at issue. It does and it is.

Since the heyday of European colonisation in the 1880s, average life expectancy and incomes have both risen, even amongst the developing nations, and have continued to do so with the upward trend most notable in the last three decades. Millions of people in India and China have made significant material gains and their vast numbers strongly influence aggregate statistics for poverty reduction. But aggregates make for poor ethics. Africa has suffered grievously during the period of 'late capitalism'.[12]

'The period of late capitalism' are weasel words, much the same historical conceit as Fukuyama's 'the end of history'. Who says it is early, late or ended? It could be argued that it arrived far too late for most Africans. The point is that during the period usually designated as 'late capitalism' the gap between per capita income in the world's richest and poorest countries has grown six-fold, and within countries spectacular differences between the richest 10% and poorest 10% have persisted and grown, again sharply since the 1970s.[13] The problem, indeed a defining feature of the global economy, is this gross inequality between the top and bottom percentiles of world society. The gap is growing. The scandal is that this is now tacitly accepted by some planners, despite millennium development targets, as the necessary price for material progress. Whether the majority of the world's population agrees with this judgement will determine just how late is 'late capitalism'. Christians cannot agree with it if they are true to their tradition.

The numerical evidence about the growth of inequality is much clearer than about the eradication of poverty. The latter has to take into account what a dollar will buy in different economies, whether individual, household or national wealth is being measured, whether like is being compared to like, median or average, and so on.[14] Taking the USA and UK as leading instances of the global upward shift in production and level of trade, while inequality fell sharply in the 1940s, and then fluctuated for three decades, during the Reagan–Thatcher years it jumped impressively. The gap between the assets of the rich and those of the poor widened rapidly during the 1980s. By the end of the decade, about one third of US workers were earning 'poverty-level' wages. Production and non-supervisory employees saw their weekly income decline from $327 in 1973 to $265 in 1990 (taking the 1982 dollar as baseline), with longer working hours and less job security, while the salaries of chief executives soared. By 1995 the assets of the top 1% of US society amounted to *c*. 40% of the country's wealth.[15]

The proportion of households in poverty in the UK, measured by the number of households with less than half the national average income, rose from 8% in 1979 to 20% in 1990. It has remained high, over 14 million people in the UK, ever since, though the Clinton and Blair governments' policies of 'making work pay', together with targeted anti-poverty measures, particularly in Britain, temporarily resulted in this rise levelling off. Nonetheless, overall inequality remains high as top-management grades enrich themselves with unashamed greed, and poverty intensifies for the least well off amongst those below the 50% poverty line. The current degree of polarisation within society is, of course, even more stark in some developing countries such as Brazil and South Africa. In short, during the recent wave of globalisation the more egalitarian 'middle' has not held; the 'middle' is being eroded as more people move into the poorest or richest 20% of society.

The reasons for this polarisation are multiple. Most obviously, in the North a political and legislative assault on weakened trades unions put organised labour into retreat during the 1980s; bargaining power weakened as industry shrank and the service and financial sectors with their use of casualised or contract workers grew. The principal dilemma for the unions was choosing between job losses or reduced wages. Unemployment in the European Union – where unlike the USA more powerful unions blocked decreases in wages – grew in the 1980s and only stabilised in the mid-1990s. The information technology revolution itself generated a dual workforce: a small group of highly skilled and highly paid software programme designers and computer specialists, alongside a much larger 'generic' group of keyboard operatives engaged in a limited number of learnt routine operations.

This weakness of labour compared to its heyday in the industrial age of mass production, and the attendant growth in inequality, was exported far beyond the powerhouse of the information economy in the OECD countries. So today, through the international division of labour, growth in inequality is distributed through a patchwork of rich and poor regions both *within* states as well as *between* states throughout the world. The geography of this global patchwork can be closely correlated with the development of highly productive nodes in the information network.

Today the network society links up concentrated nodes of technology, financial management, high skills and education, expertise in information processing, wealth, power and privilege. People and places have become differentiated into 'high value, low value and no value', with the differences reflected in everything from property prices, investment and income, to health, schooling and life expectancy. For every Silicon Valley, City of London and Ile de France, there are feeder foothills and a hinterland of isolated, disconnected and productively barren land.

The network society co-exists with the threatening black holes of marginality.[16] These of course vary in intensity of suffering. There is the absolute poverty, misery and deprivation of the majority in several African countries and then again the plight of the inner-city poor in the USA locked into relative poverty. Tom Wolfe's *Bonfire of the Vanities* captures these interacting worlds for New York and made it basic reading for the 1990s. What these black holes share, as outlined earlier, is the inability of the vast majority of their inhabitants to escape from their social and economic predicament, coupled with widespread despair and loss of hope.

The nodes of this new network map are obviously key features for the cartographers of the future – but no less is their hinterland with its apartheid of poverty. New York, London, Frankfurt, Paris, Tokyo, Hong Kong, Zurich and Los Angeles are 'global cities' in their ethnic mix, outreach and network connections. They have acted as an economic magnet over many years attracting new and massive flows of people from 'low to high-value' sites and occupations, drawing in wave after wave of immigrants. But truly prodigious urbanisation has only occurred recently and into the vast mega-cities and urban conglomerations of the Third World such as Manila, Rio, Bombay and Durban. The low value of agricultural production and lack of state support for the sector has been the push factor. Even export crops with a big market, such as coffee, suffer from overproduction and punitive prices for producers.[17]

Rural poverty accounts for the mass movement to the cities and export processing zones (EPZs) of the Third World, into different forms of informal urban trade and low-technology industrial production, much of it supplying multinationals. The migrants have been obliged to pay dearly for their modest ambitions. US senator Richard Gephart aptly described the EPZs on the Mexican border, known in Latin America as *maquiladores*, as 'twenty-first-century technology combined with nineteenth-century living and working conditions'.[18] This constant availability of cheaper labour for important sectors of industrial production, shoes and clothing for example, in the developing world and eastern Europe, has contributed – but only contributed – to de-industrialisation in the OECD. The OECD has seen a rapid growth in other low-paid jobs created by information processing, for example, keyboard operatives, retail outlets and workers in call centres. However, the dynamics of each national economy has in the main been the dominant factor in changing its employment profile, rather than the availability of cheap labour in poorer countries.

Differences of culture and language, frontier guards policing draconian immigration controls, xenophobia, nationalistic labour unions – and poor health – all limit labour's mobility across borders for those escaping the developing world. In consequence international movement is far less than might be expected. The UNDP calculates that in 1999 there were from 130 to 145 million documented immigrant workers around the world, up from 84 million in 1975. With at least some half a million undocumented economic migrants coming into the European Union alone per annum, the UNDP figure represents the tip of the iceberg. Yet, even so, this is a small amount of movement given the total global and European population, and significantly less than past waves of immigration from smaller populations, for example from Europe to the USA at the turn of the twentieth century.

It is not, of course, insignificant in terms of remittances in foreign currencies to some of the poorest countries. Nor is it insignificant as a theme for mobilising support for right-wing ultra-nationalism against asylum seekers. Indeed pressure of this kind is pushing some political parties of the centre defensively towards coded racist and xenophobic discourse and measures. Freedom of movement across state borders into Fortress Europe is circumscribed. In short, a notable feature of the most recent period of globalisation is that capital flows freely, but labour confronts a multiplicity of constraints imposed by the nation-state. There are nodes and hinterlands but geographical frontiers and the ideology of the nation-state matter. There is free trade in goods but no cross-border freedom for human labour – and contemporary economic elites intend to keep it that way.

It must be said that Karl Marx in the Communist Manifesto showed remarkable prescience when he castigated the new class of industrial capitalists of his day. And here is perhaps the profoundest continuity between new and old epochs, between the industrial and information ages: the political goals of the dominant class. 'It has resolved personal worth into exchange value, and in place of the numberless indefeasible chartered freedoms, has set up that single, unconscionable freedom – Free Trade.'[19]

The fetish of free trade, the links of the network society, the unregulated flows of capital are meant to cross all the cultures on this planet. Today they sever the local from the global, the rich from the poor, to the detriment of excluded millions, and they ensure that profit is put before people. There is no basis for integral human development here for, whatever the Coca Cola adverts portray, such a system cannot create inclusive communities in which people are valued and virtues nurtured. As Thomas Aquinas saw clearly, human identity is incomplete outside a community that encompasses all humanity in its rich diversity and locality. That is one reason why Christians celebrate the Eucharist. Meanwhile, the desire for completeness breaks out in perverse and ideological distortions, in different forms of identity politics that do violence to human history and go against its grain.

The continuing salience of Marx's reflection today indicates that resistance to globalisation must not simply analyse history, but change it, by finding a form of a political resistance that encompasses all humanity. This demands a political project that removes the obstacles to the development of human capabilities and restores personal worth. Communism tried and grievously failed. A new ethical politics with a purified and more humble sense of destiny is needed. This must radically reform the global economy in the interests of the poor, or fail. There is no better time than now as the global economy falters after 11 September 2001 and all the 'road maps' are being torn up. The next chapter looks at how, and whether, contemporary forms of resistance are meeting this challenge and their significance for the future.

CHAPTER 6

RESISTANCE MOVEMENTS

What have been described in the last three chapters are the origins and moral consequences of our misshapen global economy. This is the unpalatable human geography of our globalising world, the snapshot kept out of the album. The conventional ethical language of human rights cannot do justice to this shadow-land. The problem exceeds the capacity of individual states to offer redress. It amounts to a persistent abuse of structural power, the shaping of global structures for narrow self-interest and advantage, without concern for the common good.

The concept 'structures of injustice' first appeared in the encyclicals of Pope Paul VI conveying the idea that it is not only individuals who are unjust. We create and retain structures and networks that enact injustice and enmesh us in them. Catholic social teaching was reacting to the moral complexity of the post-colonial world, later calling the diffuse responsibility for the evil consequences of structural power – with one eye on communism – 'structural sin'.[1] I got an insight into what it could mean *in extremis* during the apartheid years when I watched helplessly as a South African youth gang broke away from the funeral of a police victim to 'necklace' a suspected collaborator.

This idea of being enmeshed in an 'involuntary' structural injustice foreshadows the contemporary theme of 'institutional racism', an accusation that cannot be countered by saying that not everyone in the institution is a racist. That is not the point. Certain structures condense and dispense injustice. That is how they operate. Apartheid was a good example, a structure of injustice that held a whole society. You either resisted or were complicit. Morally there was no middle way.

Structures have their own dynamics and life, and these can be malign. Imagine living in a Sicilian village in which all relationships revolve around the Mafia. From a moral perspective it is impossible to find a satisfactory *modus vivendi*. The only moral response to unjust structures is resistance. Many people, seeing who gains and loses from globalisation, and watching how it intensifies the apartheid of inequality, see it in this light. They opt for resistance. But to what exactly and how?

The minimal account of globalisation is the process and ideology leading to a global economy. The maximal account is an epoch change from industrial to informational societies with profound cultural changes. Both leave a lot of scope for discussion on how to react. The strategy of resistance to each is still wide open to debate. This said, we are facing today a similar analytic dilemma to the German sociologist Max Weber who, a century ago, looked back on the past century, at the transformation of agricultural Europe and the depredations of the industrial revolution, and worried about where things were heading. What were the primary causes and inner dynamics of the disruptive capitalist economy, the Beast that seemed to be driving contemporary history? Weber wanted to know if there was a meaningful connection – *sinnhaften Zusammenhang* – between the spirit of capitalism and ascetic Protestantism. Historical questions about the transition to capitalism soon brought him to confront religion and drew him into the fuzzy ideas of causality we now find in sociological theory.[2]

Weber's problem rings bells today. Indeed Castells, his intellectual successor, with his grand theory of network and information society discussed earlier suggests the first step towards mastering the Beast – understanding it. And this, in turn, leads on to some pressing questions, not least about religion. Is there a link between globalisation and the rise of religious fundamentalism? This is the burning question of the day. It could be posed less directly. Do contemporary economic changes, sharing the same time frame and geography as significant new political, social and cultural practices, allow us to talk about something more than an accidental accompaniment? Do they add up to what might be called a defining historical impulse to which reactions take religious forms?

Castells obviously thinks so, as do many other analysts who take it for granted.[3] But how? Such an impulse might shape societies by defining the dynamics of inclusion and exclusion, in other words by both attraction *and* repulsion. Weber believed that ascetic Calvinism with its work ethic was attracted to the entrepreneurial spirit that created and encouraged capitalist accumulation. They had an 'elective affinity' with each other. Might the relationship between globalisation and different forms of religious fundamentalism be the opposite, some form of repulsion? Perhaps, but it cannot be taken for granted, as it often is, without evidence.

Globalisation evidently has the potential to attract into its nodes and networks a new elite, mobile, cosmopolitan, information-rich and computer literate. What seems to be happening is that such people, defined by inclusion in a world of virtual reality, at home with an individualist ethic, accommodate themselves comfortably to a fragmented post-modernist, consumerist world. Conversely this world excludes other classes of people, the poor, illiterate, unskilled and marginalized. Are there other world views and ethics, with groups of people 'bearing' them who, for a variety of reasons, are repelled by what they experience of globalisation, and constrained to resist it? And does such an 'elective repulsion' amount to a defining counter-impulse that forms, shapes and mobilises them culturally and politically? Or are we looking under the wrong bush?

It is tempting to reduce some forms of resistance to globalisation to such a reaction to the global political economy. The success of different kinds of 'identity politics' such as religious fundamentalism is attributed to the growing poverty of the majority in polarised societies, and to high levels of inequality and disappointment with existing forms of governments. Yet the class of people most attracted and mobilised by such ideas are often not the poorest and most powerless, but aspiring literate men in employment such as minor state officials, journalists, teachers and engineers. Some, often the most mobile with experience of travel, provide not simply the leadership but the core cadres of new forms of ethnic and religious movements. It is a particular experience of the *cultural* dimension of the political economy of globalisation, its values, that seems to be their spur to resistance.

For one of the characteristics of today's globalising economy is that commodities are bought and sold ostentatiously wrapped in packages of values. Nike shoes, for example, are not only presented as useful manufactured goods to spare the feet; they are marketed as bearers of utopian fantasies about health and sport and well-being.[4] In a neo-liberal economy, it is impossible to fence off protected cultural enclaves from such values. This exposure to the diffusion of consumerist culture and Hollywood's 'revolution of rising expectations' is a key feature of the dominant economy. The gardens of the soul are everywhere overlooked by billboards, satellite television channels and the foreign images of the cinema and computer screen bearing a dominant culture into innermost recesses. Advertisements for ice cold Coca Cola, redolent of youth, vitality, happiness and the wealth of the United States, look down on societies where only the rich can afford clean water. And so on for the range of branded global products. Apples in the Garden of Eden, there is no escaping knowledge of them and the culture that they bear, and no escaping knowledge of their corollary, the nakedness and humiliation of those living in the least developed nations, cast out from the Garden, with hopeless wants and unfulfilled needs.

I have some sympathy for the American political scientist Samuel Huntington. His contentious essay on the 'Clash of Civilisations' has been rightly but roughly criticised for containing 'essentialist' understandings of 'civilisations' that implicitly ignore the importance of diversity and actual practice within them.[5] It sparked off the Iranian-led 'Dialogue of Civilisations' that ironically seems to share some of its premises.[6] There are many Islams and many Christianities and they are changing as this is written. Nonetheless, Huntington is surely right in pointing to culture as a neglected dimension of contemporary conflict, at least as a self-fulfilling prophecy in the context of globalisation. Conflict over entertainment, music, cinema and sex are but the most obvious manifestations.

The power of the neo-liberal market culture, its ability to assimilate and destroy, is truly prodigious. Capitalism can deal with diversity. True, it is a production problem – goods have to be modified and tailored to special cultural markets in flexible production, and this may reduce the productivity gains of new technology. But diversity is above all a new marketing opportunity. Ethnic foods: chapatis made in Mexico from US grain are exported and sold in

India. Genetic material, art and music: all hoovered up for commercial gain from every corner of the globe – and note how successful brand names break into our language, becoming common usage. Religious faith: check out the market for religious ideas in the New Age bazaar. That there should be movements of resistance to this juggernaut, closing windows, digging cultural trenches against 'decadence', defending dying languages, defining what is development, asserting a right to meaning and a personal identity that is beyond branding, is not surprising. Likewise that it should be the less than powerless, those who can compare, think and act their way out of their unfolding historic humiliation, who are attracted to resistance rather than fatalism.

At the very least, the 'world image' of globalisation, the new map of the world with its various subjective interpretations, might be expected to 'switch' pre-existing movements into new tracks and new dynamics. Some movements, with their specific cultures, discourses and goals clearly have been switching into new forms of political action. Whether or not these new tracks, from Al-Qa'ida to the Countryside Alliance, are best interpreted as 'resistance to globalisation' is less important than charting their impact on the policies and processes that make it up, and, in key instances, the spiral of violence that is its legacy.

At times, fearing the hegemony of the USA, governments themselves have resisted the policies that promote globalisation – for example French defence of their cinema. But in the main it has not been government but civil society, the 'sphere of social and political participation in which citizens' groups, social movements and individuals engage in dialogue, debate, confrontation, and negotiation with each other and with various governmental actors', that has spawned the most consistent and radical forms of resistance. These have taken a number of forms. The two most influential are the INGOs, the international non-governmental organisations, and violent forms of fundamentalist movements. In what follows both will be described as civil society organisations (CSOs).[7]

CIVIL SOCIETY AND ITS DISCONTENTS

If peaceful opposition to policies designed to promote neo-liberalism counts as anti-globalisation, then throughout the late 1980s and early 1990s something akin to such a movement was in formation. The first Teach-In of the International Forum on Globalisation took place in New York in 1995. This was the year Shell proposed to sink its Brent Spar platform in the Atlantic while Ken Saro-Wiwa with eight Ogoni leaders were executed by the military regime in Nigeria after protesting against the exploitation of oil resources in Ogoniland by Shell's Nigerian subsidiary. The multinationals, Disney, Nike, Gap, McDonalds were soon being challenged across a broad front on the exploitative labour practices of their supplier companies, many based in *maquiladores*. The 'sweatshop campaigns' tied in with a militant US trades-union tradition. They and the environmentalists found a powerful weapon in consumer boycotts using the purchasing power of the US universities and municipalities. By the end of the decade the multinationals were responding to the pressures from a burgeoning campus student movement: damage to their image and loss of sales. They were not long in introducing self-regulating codes of conduct.[8]

Nor was it long before the international development agencies got in on the action. CIIR, for example, used its links with the labour movement in the Philippines and with British companies to attempt to negotiate agreements on independent monitoring of Asian labour conditions. Inevitably, led by the richer and more powerful – therefore usually – northern CSOs, this branch of the movement combined a degree of co-ordination with an Internet-style networking. It concentrated on the big brand names and 'ethical shopping' through fair-trade certification, opening up the moral dimension of 'globalisation' to a domestic audience through companies and products known locally.

Meanwhile, CSOs in developing countries, particularly in Asia and Latin America, were very rapidly expanding their research base and potential for advocacy. Many were adopting a hard-line stance against neo-liberalism and globalisation. Their interest in western consumer and ethical shopping was tangential to – often – popular democratic or socialist efforts to shore up their side of the class struggle through more effective worker organisation. Their interest in 1968-style anarchist groups such as Reclaim the Streets was, to put it mildly, minimal.

Moreover, much persistent advocacy in the North was not against specific neo-liberal policies as such; indeed, in some cases, it sought *purer* neo-liberal practice on the principle of what was sauce for the goose was sauce for the gander. Lobbying in favour of unprotected Third World farmers against subsidies provided to European farmers by the European Common Agricultural Policy (CAP) might be described in this way. Though advocacy for debt remission went closer to the economic bone. Much of structural adjustment was designed to enable countries to repay outstanding debt as they faltered towards default.

Challenging CAP subsidies on the grounds of the damage caused to Third World farmers encountered a number of difficulties. Not least was the perennial economic problem of teasing out, disaggregating, the impact of CAP policies on vulnerable agricultural economies from that of other neo-liberal policies and variables. To demonstrate with clear empirical research the negative effects on local economies, say, of 'dumping' cheap food traded by agri-businesses in developing countries was difficult.[9] Common sense suggested that flooding vulnerable markets with cheap subsidised foreign food must be damaging for local producers. It required little imagination to guess the consequences of dumping European Union beef at 30 pence a kilo into southern Africa when it cost £1 a kilo to produce: some 70% of the local canning industry used imported beef.[10] But the victims, the local farmers, also suffered from a lot of other no less debilitating problems, lack of transport infrastructure, distance from markets, lack of technology, lack of inputs and so on.

There was little doubt, though, about the broad-brush results of trade liberalisation. The World Bank itself estimated that some 60% of people in the developing world benefited from trade liberalisation while the remaining 40%, some two billion, were adversely affected. When India removed barriers to foreign soya beans and edible oil in 1998, imports of these products surged by 300% resulting in an estimated loss of 1.5 million jobs in its oil extraction industry. After the NAFTA (North American Free Trade Area) agreement in 1994, 1.78 million Mexicans were forced off the land; some 40% of pig farmers and 24% of the potato farmers gave up in the face of cheap imported produce. Similar surges in agricultural imports around the world followed in the wake of the Uruguay Round of the GATT with little sign that the developing world was able to benefit by increasing its own export volume.[11] But the consequences of changes in trade were different for consumers, the urban poor, large farmers, small farmers and industrial workers. Small farmers suffered the most. Land ownership became concentrated in the hands of richer farmers and migration into towns intensified as a result. Town dwellers, of course, demand cheap food. So were CSOs speaking only for small farmers?

Another lobbying problem for the CSOs was the different relationships of European farmers to the civil society of each of their countries, and the different dynamics of the agricultural lobby in the member states of the European Union. This was often reflected in the positions taken up by national CSOs. For example, small-farm agricultural France had its champions in a number of French CSOs, and it was clear that only large farms were going to weather major CAP reform easily. Yet another problem was the growing volume of food aid passing through development agencies as the frequency of 'emergencies' grew.[12] This could also seriously distort local markets, and undermine local farmers, raising supplementary questions about grain reserves, sustainable agriculture and the impact of purchasing grain outside the region.

In practice, despite increasingly sophisticated and well-presented analyses of the issue based on detailed knowledge of the complex subsidy system, CSOs were essentially reformist in approach. They said in short that things were unfair, that the most powerful team kicked the ball downhill, and that subsidies should go. Broad practical proposals as to how to change this state of affairs were progressively added: forms of 'special and differential treatment' and 'Green Box' exemptions for the developing world were within the bounds of the politically feasible. CSOs were increasingly forced during the 1990s from thundering denunciation of government policies to policy prescription. But, of course, the US, the most powerful government team at any negotiations, was influenced by massive corporations such as Cargill, the world's largest oilseed trader and agribusiness, which in 1999 was operating in 72 countries with an annual turnover of US $45 billion.[13] Given this level of corporate clout, getting CSO policy prescriptions heard, and opening a serious review of trade policy in the light of environmental and developmental standards, was not easy.

The ideology of the 'level playing field' remains one of the most serious blockages to substantive debate. The image suggests a common sense state of affairs that easily might be achieved. But CSOs are thereby drawn into the ideological framework of neoliberalism. An awareness of the consequences of inequality and absolute poverty nonetheless lay at the heart of the CSO position. It was obvious that the small developing countries could not hope to compete in negotiating expertise and power with the OECD countries, and would be losers.

The argument made by the northern CSOs in the mid-1990s against the Multilateral Agreement on Investment (MAI) demonstrates the difficulty of taking advocacy beyond the basic unfairness of rich government policies. Here the key players on the playing field were the MNCs again and the developed nations, all with formidable lobbying power. Implicit, and sometimes explicit, in the CSO position was a preference for some form of state control, in this case promoting the directed capitalism of the developmental state. This 'statist' position, coupled with outright rejection of 1980s neoliberalism, represented faithfully the position of many of their southern partners who had been more deeply influenced by the traditional Left. But some others adopted a 'rejectionist' stance and found nothing positive to say about globalisation.[14]

Most northern development CSOs concluded that the Asian Tigers had achieved economic take-off despite neo-liberal prescriptions, largely through the state's firm guiding hand directing capital flows. Ministerial control over which industries would benefit from capital flows, and a set of policy prescriptions that bore little resemblance to those being robustly recommended by the IMF and World Bank, were pivotal for success. The State was highly interventionist in Asian domestic economies. For example during the 1980s, four large South Korean conglomerates, *chaebols*, which together were responsible for 84% of Korea's output, maintained a close association with government. The Japanese Ministry of Trade and Industry was considered something of a model of successful government direction. Even the 'non-intervention' policy of Hong Kong was associated with a high level of government commitment to growth and accompanied by massive public spending.

Pressure from the USA forced the South Korean government to allow banks in the local business conglomerates to borrow money freely on the international market, and thus become relatively free of government policy direction. And this, of course, was a key factor in the Korean collapse of the late 1990s as government totally lost control of capital flows. CSOs extrapolated from this experience. Agreements blocking such prudential exercise of national economic sovereignty were bad for development. In short, the USA, with its many allies on the IMF staff, was setting out to interdict the policies that had brought economic take-off to the OECD; they were 'kicking away the ladder'.[15]

Of course different CSOs also put forward distinctive arguments opposing the Multilateral Agreement on Investment (MAI) based on their discrete institutional interests, labour rights, environment, development and so on. But in late 1997, as New Labour went into a flurry of consultations after winning power, consortia of CSOs were expected to come up with joint positions to present to government. As chairman of such a hastily convened and eclectic consortium, I sat opposite Stanley Clinton-Davis, then a minister of state in the Department of Trade and Industry (DTI). Soon I was hiding my embarrassment as it dawned on him and the assembled civil servants that representatives of two leading CSOs present were advocating contradictory positions. Protection of birds, feeding the starving in Africa, saving the children and conserving the world's wildlife do not together make for concise and, at the same time coherent, co-ordinated positions on investment.

Moreover, proposals that the MAI negotiations should simply be scrapped, rather than reformed and begun again in a more Third World-friendly context such as the United Nations Development Programme (UNDP), a position advocated by at least one CSO, was not a proposal that civil servants would warm to. To discuss the MAI without openly challenging the economic premises behind it – and these were apparently shared by all who sat across the table – was a trap into which we were all doomed to fall.

The first New Labour government in the UK substantially changed the terms of engagement for CSOs by making formal partnership agreements with them for funding purposes, and instituting detailed consultations as part of government policy formulation. CSOs found themselves unexpectedly further 'upstream' in policy formation, a style of working to which they were not accustomed. But not so far upstream that the economic premises behind policy and the political economy of globalisation were up for discussion. That was for academic seminars.

Government expectations of CSO advocacy was for precise reformist proposals in the context of the changing paradigm of poverty alleviation. Or at least in the context of the changing analysis and priorities of the Department for International Development (DFID). More radical stances were generally the preserve of southern CSOs living with governments who were neither pro-poor nor respecters of human rights. Theirs was a style that, when transplanted to the North, the European Commission and European governments found difficult to accommodate, and which could shut down dialogue. 'Third World partners' new to the niceties of consultation could engage in the most vituperative of attacks on crusty officials in Brussels. Watching representatives of a Filippino CSO snapping at the ideological heels of stolid German and Flemish bureaucrats offered a furtive pleasure, but in the longer term it was counter-productive. The ground rules for successful consultation and advocacy were that the CSO participants blend in with the paintwork in the corridors of the European Commission while adopting the conversational cadences of *Waiting for Godot*.

Lengthy government–CSO discussions occurred throughout 2000 in preparation for the UK's Department for International Development's White Paper *Eliminating World Poverty: making globalisation work for the poor*. By this time, as the title implied, textbook neoliberal orthodoxy was sounding the retreat – though not necessarily retreating. The final version of the White Paper converged on the position of the 'reformist' CSOs. However, it contained a somewhat irenic view of the solidity of the international financial architecture and the workings of the international financial institutions. Convergence created a problem for the CSOs. They needed to sharpen their differences from government for campaigning purposes but, in truth, for the CSO reformists, the differences were not great.[16]

CLAIMING THE STREETS

Few visitors to ministerial conference rooms, even by 1997, would have called themselves part of an 'anti-*globalisation*' movement. The label was stuck on by the mass media after an extraordinary number and diversity of interest groups clogged the streets around the November 1999 WTO ministerial conference in Seattle, over 60,000 people, delaying its opening. Add some broken windows and over-reaction from police and this was headline news. The groups attending subsequent demonstrations around key international meetings of the IMF, WTO and G8 had little in common but the label. And the label certainly did not accurately reflect the position of the many reformists who were more interested in defining the direction of globalisation than ending it.

The new, loose – and amorphous – 'coalition' of environmental and labour rights INGOs, trades unions, student bodies and Churches had a penumbra of anti-capitalist political groups together with protesters against the 'global brands' such as McDonalds and Coca Cola. The street crowds continued to win Press recognition and coverage through the violent antics of the small and marginal anarchist groups (Genoa) and violent local police (Seattle and Genoa). So the Press got their modicum of newsworthy violence. But on the inside pages some of the protestors' issues got aired. The irony was that the summoning of many different groups, not by bells but e-mail, was an epiphenomenon of modern globalisation, or, at least, of its technology, the communications revolution. The same was true to a lesser degree of the campaign against landmines – branded by Princess Diana – that resulted in the signing by 121 countries of the 1998 Ottawa Landmines Convention, limiting but not abolishing their use.

These street protests had a different shape to the more successful debt-remission lobby, its principal progenitor. The movement for debt reduction for the lowest income countries, the Jubilee campaign, was a harbinger of resistance to globalisation through its focus on international finance. By ably presenting a concise ethical problem and proposing a relatively precise solution, it attracted a wide constituency, many for the first time, onto the streets. A coalition of some hundred CSOs ran a four-year campaign up to, and beyond, the millennium to cancel the $375 billion debts of the world's 52 least developed and most heavily indebted nations. British based, the campaign became more – though fractiously – co-ordinated internationally from 1998 to 2000. In the level and importance of Church involvement it was comparable to that of the Clapham sect in the anti-slavery movement. With parallel support from the British government, the campaign made a considerable impact and helped push debt to the top of the international development agenda. By staging a large street event with 70,000 people around the 1998 G8 meeting in Birmingham, it set the precedent for the waves of street protest around international meetings that followed.

However, success has been limited. Despite promises from the G8 of an agreed net total of $110 billion relief 'somewhere down the road', the reality is proving to be barely half this, spread over a number of years, and for only 22 'qualifying' countries. The debt servicing – money paid annually in interest – of the 52 most indebted countries today amounts to more than $23 billion per annum and this will be reduced by only 3.4% if the G8 stick to their debt relief. Measured by the number of people in potentially eligible debt-burdened countries who might get some benefit from this relief, assuming improbably that the opportunities afforded their governments by this remission are grasped, this amounts at best to 20% of what the lobby was seeking. A rough estimate would be a total of $35 billion in debt relief over time. Even if this amounts mainly to money that could never have been repaid, it amounts to a great deal more than charitable donations and project-funding of all the world's Third World charities put together.[17]

The northern CSOs have been trying to ease their 'Jubilee' constituency into their 'fair trade' campaign. However, the UK Trade Justice Movement lacks many of the sharp edges that facilitated the advocacy and campaigning of the late 1990s for debt remission. It is far more difficult to demonstrate that the least developed nations' declining share of trade, rather than 'debt bondage', can be reversed by focusing on measures undertaken by the developed world. They face too many other interconnected problems. Moreover, specific measures that would be beneficial, politically feasible, and 'sellable' to a campaigning public are less obvious. Getting governments to acknowledge in the WTO's legally binding provisions for international trade the vital importance of sustainable development and the environment would be most useful. But it is an essentially formal, rather than substantive step, unless backed up by a string of precedent-setting decisions in disputed cases.

Likewise the benefits from the WTO's 'special and preferential treatment' for the least developed countries depend on the capacity of such countries to respond to global markets, and, as a result of bad governance, this is often negligible. Even less easy to gain ground on are more general questions of the negative impact of US and European financial services, trade tariffs and subsidies, against the entrenched power of expert commercial lobbying groups. This does not stop the development agencies trying. CAFOD's framing the problem in cartoon $2-a-day Euro-cows, who earn more than millions of people, was an inspired piece of campaigning. As the example cited earlier of the African producers and the cotton market highlights, official inter-governmental development assistance in the form of new technology, government concessionary loans and, budget support – for example for education expenditure – and charitable giving through CSOs, make little sense if debt and unfair trade are destroying the preconditions for development.

Debt and trade have taken CSOs into fundamental questions of political economy, splitting them strategically, and creating loose and ephemeral coalitions around events, issues and places. Moreover, the Indian, Brazilian and South East Asian CSOs with strong economic research capacity have joined with other groups from the South, and are now better linked up with northern international CSOs. This has compounded the difficulty of reaching common positions in relation to policy prescription. Nonetheless, though a more rejectionist and 'statist' South is uncomfortable with the reformist tactics of the northern CSOs, and vice-versa, something of a global dialogue about globalisation has emerged. The dialogue is still several stages from a coherent political project.

These civil society movements, more particularly their reformist wing, have been widely applauded, even by governments, and promoted as a sign of the importance of 'global civil society', hopeful signs of peoples' participation in policy-making. And so, up to a point, they are. But civil society includes far more than respectable CSOs with limited political objectives. The picture of soft resistance in civil society to soft power has to be balanced by violent coercive forms if it is to reflect the contemporary spectrum. Religious fanatics, genocidal ethnic groups, terrorist organisations and nationalist groups without a state, associated with a wide variety of patho-logical and exclusive identities, have emerged from the womb of civil society. Many of these have no less claim to be placed in the category CSOs engaged in resistance to globalisation. The most important today, and for some time to come, are widely taken to fall under the broad sub-heading of 'fundamentalism'.

THE NEW FUNDAMENTALISMS

The term 'fundamentalism' first arose as a description of a particular set of evangelical Christian beliefs that gained ground before the First World War in the USA. These included most notably the belief that the scriptures were the word of God, and so 'inerrant', and that their role in informing the conduct of the individual Christian, saved by a direct and personal relationship to the Saviour, could be read off the text and was thus pivotal. The word's etymology evolved to take in the radical Islamic reform movements of the early twentieth century, partly because of a misconception that belief in the in-errancy of scripture carried the same weight in Islam as in Christianity, rather than being normative for all Muslims.

Then fundamentalism came to describe exclusive identities that mobilised people around a cultural and political project. This often involved the return to an imagined – though actually newly con-structed – past blueprint or vision of society, for example in India's resurgent Hindu fundamentalism. For Muslims the life of the com-munity at Medina in the time of the Prophet has always been normative for ethical conduct, though related in practice to the present in different ways. The idea that this is 'Muslim fundamen-talism' partly grew out of the misunderstanding that the political dimension of Muslim belief and practice was aberrant, rather than integral to most expressions of Islam. Finally the word came to be used loosely and pejoratively for a variety of – usually violent – forms of resurgent collective identities that threatened the modern state, such as the secessionist nationalism of sub-groups in multi-national states – usually forms of 'ethnic nationalism'.

More recently the term 'fundamentalism' has been applied to

almost any movement that is willing to challenge and override state law by 'God's law', or by obedience to 'manifest destiny' and the dictates of an imagined history, or by adherence to a fixed set of doctrines, and, if necessary, to use violence to achieve their ends. The American militia responsible for the 1995 Oklahoma bombing in which 169 died is a 'fundamentalist' movement in this sense. In the case of Milosevic's Kosovo pogroms, and the manipulation of Serbian ethnicity by the Serbian regime, or in India, where the Bharatiya Jamata Party became the vehicle for Brahmin ascendancy in the wake of Congress Party failure, 'fundamentalism' describes state-backed political forces playing on identity politics. For many, though, 'fundamentalism' now simply sums up the hidden subversive face of the 'other' and his beliefs, the stranger's religion or culture.

So, while 'fundamentalism' is devalued coinage as an analytic construct, it does give a name to a variety of movements that share telling commonalities. Many of these are the product of a second order splintering from previous identities that have lost their credibility and focus; many cling to their imagined social blueprints from the past in the face of rapid social change; many with their associated authoritarian structures create new, exclusive and communal identities that may be defended by force and anticipatory self-defence. Hamas out of Palestinian nationalism, initially with funding from the Israeli security services, Al-Qa'ida primarily out of the puritanical Wahabi form of Sunni Islam, initially with funding from the Pakistani Intelligence Service and CIA, the American militia out of the Patriot Movement in the USA are three spectacular examples.[18]

So fundamentalism is not some atavistic medieval hangover championed by benighted races. While expressed in an – often last ditch – communal stand that draws defensively on existing cultural and social resources, it constructs new ones out of its historic tradition. The Iranian revolution, for example, drew on Shi'ite themes of resistance and martyrdom, while the Ayatollah Khomeini innovated theologically and politically to legitimate his position as head of a revolutionary Muslim state. The resultant Iranian constitution was an amalgam of modern views of popular sovereignty and an Islamic understanding of theocratic rule. It might be described as the first revolution of the information age. With its unexpected protagonists, the mullahs and pious poor of South Tehran, and its ideology, distant enough from the expected extreme manifestations of secular ideologies in the twentieth century, most were taken by surprise.[19]

Today the field remains open for identity politics based on religion and ethnicity, each with their different themes, organisation and ways of mobilising. The growth of such movements creates a crisis of democracy for existing political parties and, more deeply, calls in question the nature of politics itself. Government may respond by sub-contracting parts of civil society to legitimate and serve its governance, for example, the Wahabi movement in Saudi Arabia in one way, and in another, as discussed later, CSOs may be drawn into collaborative reformist strategies with governments in the North. In this context, northern CSOs find themselves unable to sustain broad political projects because of their configuration as fragmented interest groups, albeit clustered in loose coalitions. Their only way forward into politics as a global 'interest group' is, like the European Greens, to morph into a local/national political party and develop a more comprehensive programme, thus becoming more electable by adopting a broad political manifesto. A similar path was taken by part of the Islamist movement in Turkey by turning into the Justice and Development Party (AKP).[20]

The Workers' Party in Brazil might then be analysed as the last transformative movement of the industrial age. But on closer inspection it offers a complex picture. Its roots were initially in the industrial unions – Lula was based in the metalworkers. But it also drew support from the activist Church and Trotskyite groups (known incidentally as the 'Shi'ites') and from NGOs. Most notably it was supported by the landless rural workers movement (MST) and by a body of liberation theologians. Victory in the Presidential elections hinged on Lula's ability to widen his base to include the middle class. This required canny concessions to globalised economic power, an ideological shift to the centre to create a winning coalition. Whether or not such inclusive coalition building can withstand future pressures and sustain a pro-poor project, evidently the hope of millions of impoverished Brazilians, remains to be seen. His period of office started well with a symbolic cancellation of a military contract to provide money for a 'freedom from hunger' campaign. 'Third Way' strategies will always be more problematic in peripheral economies, even ones with Brazil's potential than in, say, Britain. Whatever the outcome though, Brazil does not realistically promise a revolutionary transformation in the making, nor, despite the Workers' Party support for alternative social summits at Porto Alegre, the vanguard of state resistance to globalisation.[21]

So, to return to the basic question, if an important part of what is called fundamentalism today is categorised as a new politics of resistance, what exactly are fundamentalists resisting? The usual answer is 'modernisation'. However, the Iranian revolution, while drawing on the Islamic blueprint of seventh-century Medina, clearly saw itself as defining its own 'modernity'. The question becomes what is in this suspect package marked 'export modernity'?

When 'modernisation' is unpacked, it turns out to contain several key elements of 'globalisation'. Most notably for the Iranian revolutionaries, those elements with a strong ethical or political content: exported Hollywood values and culture, the collapse of the patriarchal family and other ramifications of feminist advance, the failure of existing secular nationalist projects to generate well-being. But no less, and positively, the Iranian revolution sought to derive political meaning and identity from the practice of communal Islamic principles in everything from economics to foreign policy. Identity and meaning were to be found in adherence to Islamic practice.

ISLAM AS RESISTANCE

'Fundamentalist' Christianity and Islam express themselves differently because the two world religions adopted different structural configurations to deal with the question of authority. This was largely determined by their historical origins. Ernest Gellner, an outstanding European scholar and sociologist, highlighted a scripturalist, puritan and universalist-individualist strand in both religions. It was at the core of Islam, at the heart of its high culture. Its place at the core of Christianity, at least until the Reformation, was taken by elements that had moved to Islam's periphery: what he claims are the 'hierarchy, organised mediation, bureaucratised ritual and magic' of popular religion. In Islam the latter was kept at bay by the reformist zeal of the scripturalists.[22]

This generalisation might be contested, but the broad thesis is instructive: the two world religions operate systemically with the same polarities weighted and positioned differently. From the unresolved conflict between scripturalist and hierarchical poles, between periphery and centre of Christianity, emerged secularity. But the perennial reform movements of Islam resolve the same tension in favour of its high scripturalist culture. At least on the face of it and until recently.

The difference in how this polarity is positioned and weighted has consequences for how – human – authority works in the two world religions. In Islam it is diffused because of the dominance of its scripturalist pole. Any Muslim scholar can interpret Qu'ran authoritatively, albeit within the framework of previous traditional interpretations – hence the observation that Islam does not have a clergy, rather religious specialists. These are expert in elaborating the nature and content of divine guidance for Muslim life – but on the basis of scholarship rather than assigned roles in a hierarchy. In some ways this leadership structure is comparable to the spiritual and administrative direction of certain forms of evangelical Christianity. These, of course, were also positioned as a – threatening – periphery to the 'mainstream' Churches by the end of the twentieth century.

Indeed, as a result of their lack of hierarchy and strong structures of central authority, both Islam and, to a lesser degree, evangelical Christianity had a problem in formulating a unified response to nationalism, coming to terms with it, and acting at a national level. Some Latin American evangelical Churches overcame this in the 1990s, and went so far as to put forward their own political candidates for national elections.[23] But Islam frequently came off worse than the mainstream Churches, Orthodox, Roman Catholic, Lutheran, Anglican and Methodist, in dealing with the colonial or nation-state. The lack of national hierarchies and clear authority structures to negotiate with government has been a handicap though some Islamic nationalist parties were effective in anti-colonial struggles. Islamic national-level organisations began to exert effective pressure for Muslim interests in most sub-Saharan African states only in the early 1970s.[24] In short, Islam has rarely formed a potent amalgam with 'fundamentalist' ethnic nationalism in the same way as the Christian Churches; the Chechens are a new development. The instances of the Basques, Irish, Croats, Timorese, Poles and Serbs have few Islamic parallels.

Yet, even with Islamic Councils, university and youth organisations, new authoritative judgements on matters of politics and ethics binding on all are a problem; the *ulama* are not a hierarchical priesthood or organised ministry and do not act like one. Nor was the idea of the nation-state historically incorporated easily into Islamic theology with its emphasis on a universal community, the *umma*, and the sovereignty of God, *Hakimiyyat Allah*. This, though, on the upside has allowed a great deal of flexibility and a variety of political responses to globalisation.[25]

Buoyed up by oil wealth and international support, by 1974 Islamic groups were pushing strongly – but initially unsuccessfully – for a Shari'a Federal Court of Appeal in Nigeria, a country where Muslims were not in a clear majority.[26] From the 1990s one northern state after another imposed Shari'a law in the face of Federal disapproval and Nigerian Christian opposition. The secular Turkish state and *'pancisila'* Indonesia with its constitutional recognition of the country's different religions, both authoritarian regimes, were able to contain these pressures despite large and predominantly Muslim populations, but both have recently encountered a resurgence of Islamic militancy and, in Indonesia, a fundamentalist political project. The Justice and Development Party (AKP), which won the 2002 Turkish elections, developed from an Islamic movement and campaigned on themes of social justice and improvements for the poor. This responded to a deep debilitating recession and widespread disillusion with the secular ruling Party. By way of contrast, there is little doubt that the Jemaat Islamiya, founded in the early 1970s in Indonesia, has now been infiltrated by Al-Qa'ida cells.

The success of Islam as a political project lies both in its capacity to promote a strong cultural counter-force to what are seen as western 'values' – or lack of them – and in this flexibility of its political response. It can present itself as the answer to secularism's failure to create just societies and, Christianity being seen as compromised, as the only response to perceived ethical failures in the West. Though exclusive in the strong sense of defining the enemy, and in the weak sense of dividing people into Muslims and non-Muslims, it has a great capacity to assimilate across cultures. The traded goods and brand names of the global economy, computer technology, nuclear physics, are all potentially grist to the mill of building a modern Muslim society. It winnows out what is acceptable and useful from what is not, offering a culture to the weak, strong enough to assimilate the powerful artefacts of the West. Fundamentalism in this context appears as a form of defensive 'modernisation', a counter-project to western-dominated globalisation.

My own experience in Iran is that Islam is systemically and structurally adapted to 'fundamentalism' only in this sophisticated defensive sense.[27] The pressures of globalisation merely triggered an inherent dynamism towards building an integral Muslim identity. But many sections of society do not want to move down that track and there is a hidden pluralism within Islam. The possibilities of the communications revolution allow Muslim diasporas to build new political movements on the basis of new interpretations of the Qu'ran that sweep aside the traditional teaching of the *ulama*. The vast majority of Muslims today are not trying to impose an integral Islamic politics and ethics derived from the sacred texts of the Qu'ran and sayings of the Prophet on the multicultural societies in which they live. Some positively encourage accommodation with democracy and nationalism.[28] But some interpretations 'switch' Muslims into a radical transformative politics. What then are the systemic factors in Islam making it likely that radical fundamentalism as a project, rather than forms of co-existence and accommodation, emerges in reaction to globalisation?

Islam's inner dynamic, in as much as one can be detected historically, involves as its central project a struggle against the pagan religious culture, ritual and syncretism of agricultural societies. This religious striving, *jihad*, in the path of God, *fi sabil allah*, pitted the high literate culture of town and desert, the teachings of Qu'ran and the sayings of the Prophet, Hadith, against paganism and religious innovation. The divine guidance given in these sacred scriptures, made concrete as Islamic law in the Shari'a, prescribed this path and how to remove the obstacles on it. This dynamic of purification and struggle was, as it were, waiting to be switched into dealing with the hegemonic cultural force of globalisation and its 'Great Satan', the USA.

The slow undermining of the nation-state by processes involved in globalisation, and the rise of the network society, gives an advantage to the unique polarity and dynamics of Islam over the more 'nationalised' Christianity. Rapid urbanisation throughout the Islamic world has decisively shifted the balance in favour of the high Qu'ranic culture of civil servants, university lecturers and tradesmen in the bazaar, and thus towards privileging movements of reform and resistance. It has introduced a new generation of 'lay' scholars and, to some extent, begun to marginalize more traditional, local *ulama*. It may also have shifted the balance in favour of evangelical Christianity and Islam against adherence to the 'mainstream' Churches, it should be added.

Civil societies, which grew out of the space partly vacated by the Churches in the West, though including them, are still nationally differentiated. But, as shown earlier, they are quickly adapting to operating in a network society and information age. Islam with its – at least notionally – universalist Muslim *umma*, diffuse authority and networks of religious expertise and high culture based on university and *madrasa*, is well positioned for the new epoch. Cultural and political resistance to secularity and paganism, the touchstone of past Islamic success, has been switched onto the track of resistance to American-directed globalisation with devastating effect.

Thus militant Christians in the West find themselves alongside secular colleagues in civil society engaged in single-issue advocacy, or in coalitions against aspects of globalisation. Meanwhile militant Muslims transform their identity as opponents of secularity and paganism into that of artisans of a new Muslim society in conscious opposition to what they perceive as the West's total project, globalis-ation. Militant – non-evangelical – Christians on the whole form inclusive coalitions. Militant Muslims on the whole form exclusive communities. Only the latter have an articulated political project. And there were no more committed proponents of Huntington's 'clash of civilisations' in practice than the Iranian religious specialists who came to power in 1979, or radicals such as Dr Hasan al-Turabi in Sudan and Ali Abassi al-Madani in Algeria.[29]

Islamic movements are more able to morph into fundamentalist political parties in order to gain power and capture the state, than any configuration of secular CSOs emerging to date in western civil society. Seizure of state power on an Islamist – fundamentalist – ticket might once have seemed achievable through democratic elec-tions, ousting more traditional nationalists, or through personal ties and clientism after nationalist governments had come to power in predominantly Muslim countries. But no more. Algeria, where any possibility of fundamentalist government after victory at the polls was aborted, suffering massive human rights violations since 1991, has been a turning point. Repression in Egypt blocked other strong movements. Counter-violence was legitimated by recourse to a – what many Muslims would consider spurious – divine mandate to forge an Islamic society. Declarations of self-appointed and unchecked religious scholars to this effect are commonplace. The elaborated traditions of the local *ulama* come to be seen as replaceable by the new doctrines of popular 'lay' experts.

Though capture of state power is apparently inconsistent with the universalism of the *umma*, it is perfectly consistent if viewed as a necessary instrumental measure to establish a society based on Islamic principles. After all, these principles delineate Muslim submission to God and the obedience of the *umma*. The popularity of fundamentalist projects grows out of the popular idiom of reform and revival. It rallies its forces around the weakness of Muslim societies and the perceived 'irreligion' of their rulers. Historic humiliation, the political and material failure of the Islamic world, a widespread disappointment with corrupt national governments, and, for Muslim countries, the interpretation of this corruption and failure in terms of political leaders' straying from the path of Islamic principle, forms the heart of the matter.[30] It is a bitter legacy. But a key signifier of this perceived betrayal and diversion from the path of God today is association with the USA.

NETWORK TERRORISM: AL-QA'IDA

The most ominous seizure of power to date has proved to be the capture of the disintegrated Afghanistan state by the Taliban, and the parasitic relationship to it of Al-Qa'ida (The Base). Al-Qa'ida began as a self-selected Muslim international brigade formed in the 1980s. Their direction came largely from well-educated and well-travelled, Saudi, Egyptian, Algerian and Yemeni fundamentalists. Drawn to expel the Soviet invaders from the Middle East, they were encouraged, trained and funded by Pakistan and less directly by the USA. The resulting Al-Qa'ida network was loosely organised with a 'Shura Majlis', consultative council, and ran training camps through which passed Muslims from a number of different nationalities. These in turn, after the Afghan war against the Soviets, later formed independent cells in some 50 different countries.

The 1991 Gulf War, the continued use of Saudi Arabian territory as a US base for launching an offensive to repel Iraq's occupation of Kuwait, the aftermath of this war, sanctions, bombing and a 'no-fly zone' of dubious legality, and the plight of the Palestinians confronting ever more hard-line Israeli governments, changed the configuration of the Middle East in the 1990s. If the pronouncements of Al-Qa'ida are to be believed, all this was seen as a projection of US power, an assault on the territorial integrity of Islam, a physical attack on Muslim identity.[31]

There is no evidence that the published pronouncements of Al-Qa'ida represented anything other than the politics of the network. Interrogation of suspects after the defeat of the Taliban confirmed the principal political demands made in the 1990s. In February 1998 *al-Quds al-Arabi*, a London-based Arabic newspaper, printed an Al-Qa'ida appeal to the Muslim world signed by five of its leaders, including Osama bin Laden and Ayman al-Zawahiri, its self-appointed Muslim spokesmen. This 'Declaration of the World Islamic Front' was framed as a call to struggle against 'Jews and Crusaders', and strove to echo the language of the Qu'ran. 'The Arabian Peninsula has never . . . been stormed by any forces like the crusader armies spreading in it like locusts, eating its riches and wiping out its plantations', it began.

The theme of an imminent emergency facing the Muslim world occurred in an earlier publication by bin Laden in 1996, a call for 'collective defence' of the sacred territory of the Arabian peninsula where the Prophet founded Medina and received the divine message at Mecca. Bin Laden claimed that the Americans had attacked God, the Prophet and Islam by their actions in the Middle East. Two years on, the new call asserted that in the face of what was an extreme emergency it was now incumbent on every Muslim to defend Islam, – *fard 'ayn*, as an individual and religious duty – just as when Medina was threatened by invaders at the time of the Prophet. And defence could involve attacking the 'crusaders' anywhere in the world.[32]

This was stretching the Islamic tradition, but not beyond reasonable grounds. Islam shared with Christianity medieval theories of the just war and traditionally defined aspects of *jus ad bellum* and *jus in bello*, when it was permissible to go to war and how war should be conducted. Thus in an extreme emergency Muslims would not need the political authority of a Caliph, the head of the Muslim community, to wage war. Necessity could justify doing 'forbidden things', such as a group of individuals taking up arms and using them outside the Islamic heartland. What Islamic tradition does not countenance is, of course, terrorism. The 'forbidden things' in the text could not legitimately be interpreted as being the targeting of civilians for military and political purposes. The Qu'ran itself is explicit that attacks on innocents are not permitted. Such acts are murder. Within this tradition the attacks on World Trade Center in 1993 and on 11 September 2001 were wicked innovations, the acts of rebels – if not criminals – and certainly not Islamic.

Notwithstanding, this is not the interpretation that a tiny and dangerous minority of Muslims accept. And Al-Qa'ida benefits from the diffuse authority structure of Islam to appeal, with an assumed aura of scholarship, to culturally humiliated masses of Muslims around the world. That Islam faces such an emergency and that terrorism in this context is permitted as a last resort is believed by some of them. The 'strike a blow and die' desperation of the attacks on New York and Washington resonates with a pathological form of the psychology of the oppressed and with religious themes of martyrdom. They indicate the failure of the fundamentalist project to achieve political power by democratic means, persuasion and example.

But in their cold, calculated and precise planning the attacks indicate a deeper pathology. The targeting of a powerful symbol of the globalised capitalist economy, the World Trade Center, in a key node of the information society, was, of course, terrorism on a spectacular scale. But it was also part of a complex political project, part national, to overthrow the Saudi royal family, part ethnic, to purify the Arab world, and part global, to forge a fundamentalist and universal Islamic community and identity. The attack on the Pentagon, and what may have been a failed attack on the White House, highlighted the two symbols of the political and military power behind globalisation. By most measures, the attacks place the Al-Qa'ida network in the framework of the anti-globalisation movements of the twenty-first century. Such terrorism is the pathological shadow of the network society and the nemesis of globalisation. It is essential to treat its causes as well as its symptoms. To do so requires a deeper reflection on the emergence of civil society globally.

CHAPTER 7

GLOBAL CIVIL SOCIETY

'Atlantic society is endowed with Civil Society, and on the whole, at any rate since 1945, it has enjoyed it without giving it much or any thought.' So wrote the late Ernest Gellner, a respected theorist of European political thought, at the beginning of the 1990s.[1] But even as he wrote this was no longer true. Indeed the contrary would be more true today. Civil society is the focus of almost the same intense analysis and speculation as globalisation. Moreover, few would deny that the two very different manifestations of today's civil society, Al-Qa'ida and international NGOs, have each in their own way contributed to this interest. Both have had a profound impact on international relations. And their impact urgently raises the question of the future in the twenty-first century of what has been called 'global civil society'.

The idea of civil society returned centre-stage to political discourse at much the same time as the concept of globalisation came to prominence, at the end of the 1980s. This coincidence with the fall of the Berlin Wall was no accident; after all, it was a fettered civil society, the Churches and intellectuals such as Vaclav Havel and Adam Michnik, breaking free to lead the velvet revolutions in central Europe that heralded the end of communist government. From this point onwards 'civil society' was promoted as a shorthand for that form of association which the transitional states of the ex-Soviet Union and Eastern bloc had lacked.

Its absence came to explain the catastrophic failure of the transition to market economics in Russia and in several of its eastern

European neighbours. It provided an alibi for the neo-liberal consultants sent from the West, the inadvertent sponsors of a new class of criminals. 'Civil society' emerged in this context as an economic externality of special distinction. It explained what were described as 'transitional' problems: the lack of institutions, legal, contractual and commercial, necessary to underpin the efficient working of the market. And, at a more abstract level, the forms of association that generated trust and the other social prerequisites for sustainable economic exchanges over time and distance.

The importance of trust and what was oddly called 'social capital' – for capital is itself a socially constructed reality – was rediscovered and proclaimed by policy-makers with the enthusiasm of evangelical belief in the atonement of the Cross. But 'social capital' described little more than what Adam Smith meant by 'propriety', the practice and expectation of honest, disciplined and predictable behaviour based on shared social norms and codes. That had been considered good for the market a long time ago. However, it required the Russian Mafias to highlight its salience in modern times.

'Civil society' itself had, of course, an honourable pedigree going back to Adam Ferguson and the Scottish Enlightenment, and to Hegel, and, via Gramsci, into European Marxist thought. But the resonances of the 'civil society' referred to by Ferguson in 1767 differed from what Antonio Gramsci was concerned about from his Italian prison in the early 1930s. The blurred boundaries of the concept were key to its charms.[2]

So, this dowager duchess of an idea, a little worse for wear, returned to the political stage to rave reviews from both Left and Right. For the Left, suffering the defeat of all 'really existing socialism', save in Cuba, North Korea, Laos and some Indian states, here was a terrain of struggle on which to oppose the hegemonic ideas of a victorious globalising capitalism. For the Right, it was redolent of the Thatcher–Reagan conceits of the day: the supposedly shrinking state, a new emblem of opposition to the encroachments of big government and 'red tape', a code for the freedom of the yeoman English. It evoked homely expressions of liberty: Rotary, Round Table, Brownies and the Women's Institute. Or, across the Atlantic, School Boards, Bowling Alleys and – less cosy – Gun Clubs and Michigan Militia. 'The art of association must grow and improve among them at the same speed as equality of conditions spreads,'

Alexis de Tocqueville proclaimed on surveying democracy in America in 1845. And so it has.[3]

The new vision of civil society as ingredient 'X' in successful capitalism placed it high on the scale of developmental desiderata. It was both instrumental for development and fuzzily constitutive of it. Where it was lacking, it had to be constructed by interventions of various sorts. Where it was present it was assigned broad functions according to the legitimacy and strength of government. So, though building civil society lay at the intersection of potentially incompatible political projects, it became a widely perceived and shared 'good' to be pursued. World Bank, governments and CSOs, everyone was in favour of it. CSOs could condense new forms of opposition to corrupt and oppressive governments, act as mediating providers of services for the lean and mean modern state, and perform a range of useful, indeed necessary, functions to reduce instances of 'market failure'.

So the end of the millennium saw a return to prominence again of a widely shared social self-understanding amongst the contemporary political elite, the consciousness of living in relation to three basic organisational forms: government, civil society and the family. Each was vulnerable to powerful political critiques – though civil society got off lightly. Moreover, the intensity of the interaction between them had been growing apace in the latter half of the last century, and this raised new questions and was significant in itself. A poor family in Europe might receive the attention of several government agencies at the same time, from police to social workers, and at regular intervals. Civil society charities in the UK might provide volunteers to help families function better, or mentors for children with absent fathers. More recently, Government–civil society 'partnerships' with CSOs became the stock-in-trade of modern governance, with high levels of consultation, and a range of purposes, mirroring the vogue for public–private partnerships with business. Yet, increasingly, the interaction between these forms and their special features were viewed as problematic and politically contested.

Not surprisingly in a world of jet travel and instant communications this social self-understanding was projected beyond the nation-state to inform thinking about international relations. NGOs wished to share information and to seek allies across nation-state boundaries, engaging in joint action and campaigns on a range of problems perceived to be global in scope: environment, human rights, development, law, peacemaking. The fax and telephone bills of an organisation such as the CIIR were heavily skewed towards international calls, and the travel budget was always a major item. E-mail came as a spectacular cost-cutting advance. Programmes of work were co-ordinated across ten or more countries; campaigns and joint action could involve eight NGOs on four continents on a daily basis.

Civil society now numbers a plethora of institutions of which NGOs are an important part. One of the characteristics of the modern period of globalisation has been the massive growth in the number and form of international non-governmental organis-ations (INGOs) from fewer than 5,000 in 1972 to over 47,000 in 2001 – alongside, of course, the prodigious growth of multinational corporations (MNCs). Some 40% of INGOs are national bodies with international outreach or orientation. Others, such as OXFAM, have proliferated from a national base and reassembled in a quasi-federal structure involving several national organisations sharing the same brand name. Some, like sports federations and the Inter-national Olympic Committee, represent clusters of nationalist, with most often commercial, interests lurking behind their sports internationalism. The latter has been demonstrably corrupt.

A growing number of more recently created INGOs have adopted more experimental forms, some existing only on the Internet, or are otherwise poorly institutionalised, and a comparable number have only a limited life-expectancy.[4] Thus a process of active citizenship at the nation-state level is quickly being translated into a significant new dimension of a wider citizenship. This globalisation from below is having a sustained impact on international relations, which cannot now plausibly be understood as merely relations between states alone.

ON BREAKING THE SOCIAL CONTRACT

The reasons for this multiplication of INGOs are multiple and not simply the new opportunities afforded by the communications revolution. In the fifty years since the creation of the United Nations system, despite the best efforts of its international civil service and agencies, the world body has only patchily operated beyond and outside, in this sense transcended, the interests and constraints of its member states. The arm-twisting and diplomacy associated with achieving unanimous agreement on Security Council Resolution 1441 in November 2002, aimed ultimately by the USA at obtaining a United Nations mandate for military invasion of Iraq, illustrated the point with brutal realism. As, indeed, in the context of a culpable passivity and refusal to engage, did the international inaction after April 1994 during the Rwandan genocide. No state saw it in their interests to act – save France for the wrong reasons. The failures of a global social contract have been glaring. Many CSOs have sought to remedy them.

The distinction between an 'inter-national' and a global vision is fundamental. 'Taken together, the constitutions of the (UN) System gave humanity a comprehensive international social contract for the first time,' wrote Erskine Childers in 1994.[5] There is no shortage of international institutions created from above: at the latest count an extraordinary number, 6,743 inter-governmental organisations, up from a mere 37 at the beginning of the twentieth century.[6] The weaknesses and sins of omission of this social contract, in the dominant inter-governmental 'layer' of international relations, more than any other factor, accounts for the irruption of the INGOs as significant players on the international scene in the last thirty years.

The UN General Assembly and Security Council were intended as multilateral, consultative and executive bodies in the hope of achieving co-ordinated expressions of global responsibility and democratic governance. But, founded on a principle of national sovereignty and non-intervention, the Security Council inevitably acted as a negotiating forum in which member nation-states pursued their own interests within the constraints of shifting balances of power. Member states attempt to implement the UN Charter most often when it coincides with their perceived national interest, or, at least, when it appears to recommend action detrimental to their enemies. It was therefore naïve to suppose, as many imagined, that the euphoria at the ending of the Cold War would simply translate into a period of idealistic internationalism. Any quickening of the desire for a new international order similar to that which contributed to the founding of the United Nations in 1945 was short-lived and half-hearted.

Thus the political dynamics of the UN post-Cold War remain narrowly international, in the sense of being a significant terrain of political interaction between nation-states, rather than global, in the sense of transcending narrow national interest according to its Charter intentions: towards peace, human rights, justice and development. An influential strand of US thinking dismisses its importance in these areas, and the new US National Security doctrine of preventive war undermines its basic principles.[7] Indeed US unilateralism gained momentum during the 2003 Gulf War delivering a body blow to a UN system based on international law.

So the global quality of the UN agencies, for labour, refugees, health or development, against drugs, for example, has perennially to be striven for against a minimalist nationalist *realpolitik*. The UN's high profile work on the environment provides an essential forum for debate and joint planning that by definition transcends the confines of the nation-state but, again, it is thwarted by the USA. The little known work, for example, of the Universal Postal Union and the International Telecommunications Union is less contested though not immune to neo-liberal ideology and commercial pressures. The World Health Organisation (WHO) in a time of global pandemics encourages pragmatic responses that can be driven by simple fear as in the 2003 SARS outbreak. So it is that the UN still finds itself today the world's leading international organisation, perhaps holding an embryo of global governance within it, with heroic forms of global action taking place under its auspices, most notably in the arena of health; the WHO's successful eradication of smallpox between 1967 and 1977 is a shining example.

The question is whether an organisation whose principles are founded on national sovereignty and non-intervention – enshrined in Article 2(4) of the Charter – with the sacredness of frontiers as the trump card in its pack, can nurture the embryo of global governance? True, 'ethnic cleansing', threats to international peace and security, and grave humanitarian crises exceptionally but increasingly override the trump cards of the Charter. But by whom and how are these exceptions being defined? And do they risk, to use the words of the Secretary-General, Kofi Annan, 'undermining the imperfect, yet resilient security system created after the Second World War without a clear criterion on who might invoke these precedents'?[8]

Most immediately is not this risk to the UN heightened in the asymmetric world of a single hegemonic superpower – probably two if China holds together and gains sophisticated weaponry and comparable economic power by *c*. 2030? And would the outcome of nurturing global governance through the UN, thus hobbled, have a desirable result? For it is the historic nature of strong states not to believe that they need to pool sovereignty in multilateral organisations to achieve their national goals, and thus not to wish to do so. The bullying, selective unilateral action – and inaction – and arrogance of the USA, have become a grave international problem.

The resuscitation of NATO, the growth of regional trading blocs with, in Europe, aspirations to new forms of governance, the founding of the WTO outside the UN framework, the G8 meetings would suggest that the contemporary tide is moving against future global governance through a reformed UN. Ad hoc groupings, clubs of the willing and powerful, seem to be the order of the day. Perhaps we are better off with a diversity of bodies that may prove less easily captured ideologically by the most powerful and militaristic?

This then has been the complex background to rapid growth in the number and variety of INGOs. It is as if an equal and opposite globalisation from below is underway. As if the failures and limits of inter-governmental global governance are drawing in all those whose understanding of citizenship takes them beyond the confines of the nation-state. This does not mean the supporters of the INGOs are abandoning the United Nations. Far from it. The international peace movement, for example, has in the past decade begun to promote the United Nations strongly, more so than in the past, as have several of the more important international development agencies alongside local United Nations associations.[9]

Formal affiliation and accreditation of INGOs to the UN's Economic and Social Council (ECOSOC) is of long standing. ECOSOC has major subsidiary bodies on human rights – the Human Rights Commission in Geneva – and sustainable development. But it suffers from the full gamut of UN maladies: refusal of powerful member states to permit it to play the role for which it was originally intended, understaffing, a narrowly politicised participation from several important nation-state members – for example to requests for

ECOSOC status from INGOs – overwork, and a slow bureaucratic routine.

I once spent a leisurely two days in New York waiting to get affiliation with ECOSOC for CIIR. Advice given to me was to lobby friendly national delegates to ensure a successful application, and to watch out for vetoes. The translators arrived on time. Delegates languidly trickled in, as into a London club, over the space of an hour. Then the waiting began. Representatives of the People's Republic of China lapsed into incomprehensible tantrums on not receiving a French translation of one CSO application for affiliation, and then filibustered to stop another, a Tibetan Human Rights organisation. Supporting the UN, it seemed to me during two long sessions, was as compelling as joining 'the only game in town'.

In summary, ethical action on a global scale, increased non-military forms of intervention across frontiers is recommending itself to the conscience of many, irrespective of the sanctity of national sovereignty, and the limitations of the UN. From Burmese jails to the barrios of Latin American cities a new activist diaspora is found today drawn from a variety of ethical traditions. Such intervention is political in nature, however it is formally presented. And, were there to be some broadly shared strategy, which there is not, it would be aimed primarily at carving out a supranational sphere of social and political participation in order to tame and channel market-driven globalisation.

The ethical quest for globalisation from below must be translated into institutions and law. Immanuel Kant wrote in the 1780s of the need for a universal law of, and for, world citizenship befitting a law-governed *burgerliche* (civil) society, involving common rules and common institutions. But he saw this as coming from above, from and through states not through some form of global parliament, a United Nations of the Peoples.[10] That is not enough. And it is happening too slowly. People have to obey laws and codes of conduct for them to work. But there are precedents. The cosmopolitan ethic of the humanitarian tradition based on the rights of individuals irrespective of their nationality and territoriality, working with a premise of political neutrality and impartiality, offers a fascinating terrain on which to explore the ethical problems of globalisation from below.

HUMANITARIAN INTERVENTION

International humanitarian law has been subject to considerable tensions during the 1990s as a result of interventions from both civil society and the UN system. Important questions have arisen in the context of contemporary civil wars and UN-mandated military intervention – though they first emerged during the famines in Biafra in 1971 and Ethiopia in 1984. They introduce a broader political dimension to humanitarian intervention. Moreover, several of the interventions fall under the suspicion of using a UN humanitarian mandate as a cloak for different forms of unilateral action by member states.

Whether in Kosovo or Somalia, military interventions for humanitarian purposes have blurred the boundaries of state and civil society action. By 1988, the practice of creating 'humanitarian corridors', with armed force to protect them, had received approval from the UN Secretary-General. The major military operations of the 1990s effectively exploited this innovation to lever open more 'humanitarian space'. In such situations INGOs cannot both keep military forces at arm's length and do their job; they now often have to work with, or alongside, NATO or other armed forces to reach civilian populations. Anarchic 'civil war' and local war economies pose an additional constraint as INGOs' neutrality is inevitably called in question. Inadvertently feeding genocidal killers, depending on the firepower of Blue Helmets, or negotiating trucks past guerrilla road blocks, the aid worker cannot reasonably hope to be perceived as impartial whatever his or her intentions. There is a choice between feeding the starving and clothing the naked and preserving an impartial humanitarian space 'with consent'. For a variety of reasons, 'neutral humanitarian space' has begun to shut down.

INGOs are thus placed in a quandary. When armed intervention coincides with clear humanitarian imperatives, for example to end 'ethnic cleansing' in Kosovo, or is aimed at destroying the women-hating Taliban in Afghanistan, they may approve even when it amounts to unilateral action by the United States. The cloak of allies or mandating UN resolutions, won by twisting arms in the Security Council, is cosmetically helpful. Or they can maintain a stand against what Noam Chomsky derides as the new imperialism of 'military humanism'.

There are good grounds for saying 'no': the only chance of the UN becoming a genuine global actor is resistance to collaboration with unlawful violations of national sovereignty and de facto unilateral action. The price of a principled commitment to the intentions of the UN Charter, though, can be inaction in the face of intolerable suffering. Moreover, the stakes are raised when public opinion is mobilised for action by television images. It seems indefensibly purist to castigate the unilateral Vietnamese invasion of Cambodia in 1977, ousting the Khmer Rouge, or the unilateral Tanzanian invasion of Uganda in 1979 that ended the murderous regime of Idi Amin, in the name of the Charter's principles.

Moreover, as a result of inefficient bureaucracy and shortage of staff and funds, an unreformed UN notoriously moves slowly or not at all. The current US administration certainly wishes things to stay that way. It consistently held back over $1 billion in dues owed to the body during the 1990s. Indeed, few member states wish to risk interventions under Charter provisions for relieving acute suffering or promoting human rights. The protection of victims can prove a long and costly commitment that has to be repeated in the next trouble spot. UN Resolution 688 authorising safe havens in Iraq in 1992 notably referred to threats to peace and security rather than humanitarian concern after brutal repression of the Kurdish population by the regime in Baghdad – as did the intervention against the military kleptocracy in Haiti a year later. Who picks up the tab for reconstruction and rebuilding increasingly becomes a central question. The weakness of the UN stems from the ethical failure of its member states, a pervasive lack of will to act in the common good.

The 2003 war on Iraq raised the humanitarian dilemma in an acute form. It offered an end to tyranny and a way out of a brutal sanctions policy causing immense civilian suffering. Humanitarian sentiments were repeatedly and cynically played on by the US and Britain. This in the full knowledge that military intervention was being justified 'legally' – spuriously – in terms of UN provisions for safeguarding international peace and security. Removal of alleged weapons of mass destruction poorly concealed the real goal of 'regime change'. The threat from Iraq was not imminent and the legal justification for war stretched reason and credulity – though not that of the British

Attorney-General. Going to war without a UN mandate undermined the UN as an embodiment of international law. The calculus between long-term consequences and short-term gains, between the alleviation and creation of suffering, sharply profiled in INGO reluctance to work with the military later in Iraq, raises deeper questions of partnership with the state and its dangers.[11]

PARTNERSHIP OR CO-OPTING?

There is a plausible consensus that civil society first developed on the back of emergent 'civilised', urban, commercial life in Europe as a desirable 'condition of liberty' and a counter-balance to the state. This strand of thinking carried forward from the Scottish Enlightenment and Adam Ferguson to re-emerge with similar resonances during the collapse of bureaucratic communism. It was influential in the Latin American struggle for democratic space under the oligarchies and tyrannical US-sponsored governments of the 1980s – though carrying a distinctive political emphasis. The role of 'civil society' today, then, cannot be immune to a critical appraisal of its significance as a vehicle of countervailing 'soft power' in different contexts.

To bring the problem home into the domestic realm, government – civil society partnerships in the UK, in my experience, enhance the suspicions of southern CSOs about their sister organisations in the North. Northern CSOs might be honey-traps drawing them into reformist solutions, a human face to an economic agenda that is not in their interests. Or, more moderately, that the power and expertise of their sister organisations facilitate the imposition of unwelcome donor-led strategies for which their compliance is expected. The problem has been acute in the politicised humanitarian interventions of the last decade. The fear is that 'global civil society' will not contest the established order with its gross asymmetries of power but subtly reinforce it, by reflecting prevailing power relationships between governments. In other words, northern INGOs, as most governments desire, will inadvertently become sophisticated conduits for the foreign policy of northern governments.[12]

This is self-evidently a possibility. It is a particular danger when the foreign policy in question is, as often it will be, misguided or based on pure *realpolitik*. But to assert it as an inevitable consequence of asymmetric structural power is simplistic. It says little for the critical faculties of partner northern INGOs and their stakeholders. Many northern INGOs receive government money either in the form of grants from the European Union or from their own national government. Some 10% of overseas development assistance from the Netherlands, for example, passes through INGOs, the highest proportion amongst the major European donors except tiny Luxembourg. Indeed Amnesty International, Survival International and Greenpeace, which for understandable reasons refuse state funding, stand out. Now it is obviously preferable for INGOs to operate solely on membership income, and important to minimise the percentage of total income coming from government donors. But this does not mean that those who take the Queen's shilling are always bought – though he who pays the piper does have the *right* to call at least some of the tunes, even if the piper refuses.

Elected governments govern through the allocation of funds for purposes defined by policies in their manifestoes. When INGOs accept such funding, it is reasonable for government to expect them to use at least some of it in compliance with, or for, promoting shared policy objectives. And it is reasonable that this work should then be monitored. Here I must declare an interest. I negotiated a partnership agreed with the Department for International Development of the British government, (DFID), on behalf of the Catholic Institute of International Relations (CIIR) in 2000. One of the preconditions for accepting such funding – acknowledged by all eligible INGOs – was that advocacy critical of government policies would not be jeopardised. Moreover, it was clearly stated in the agreement where CIIR disagreed with DFID's approach. The Department was specific about what aspects of the organisation's work it wished to support, but was happy to see programmes that it did not wish to fund directly continue alongside them as normal.

Southern CSOs are right to keep such financial relationships under scrutiny. But the unstated conviction that northern INGOs ought invariably to occupy the role of de facto opposition to democratically elected political parties, so that co-operative action is inappropriate, is misguided. Whether they ought to, or not, will depend entirely on an evaluation of government policies, and to a lesser extent the remit of opposition politics. Indeed, at present, there is much to be said for *increasing* the co-operation between civil society and like-minded social democratic governments, with great care, across a range of areas in the realm of global responsibility. This cannot, of course, for a variety of reasons, extend to collaboration or association with their Intelligence agencies, not least because transparency must be one of the organisational values of NGOs – nor in many contexts with their military. But to provide impetus to a social democratic counter-force against US unilateralism is a conjunctural necessity given its current character, policies and power over international affairs.

In other words, the relationships that INGOs adopt must be determined not by universal, a priori, assumptions about the role of civil society, but stem from a prudential judgement of historical context and contemporary governance. In collapsing states and in war economies the primary task of civil society will be to work for the establishment of national governance structures. In the context of patrimonial states and corrupt government the struggle for human rights and democracy will be primary. In most instances considerable tension between state and civil society is to be expected. But in strong social democratic states the possibility of alliances for the pursuit of common goals arises. Such alliances will be less dangerous to INGO independence to the degree that the INGO has a clear vision of a wider ethical and political project to which state and civil society can contribute in their different ways. It is worthwhile to give some recent examples of where alliances have worked and their relative success.[13]

THE INTERNATIONAL CRIMINAL COURT

On a warm evening in early July 1998, I was at a reception hosted by the Human Rights unit of the British Foreign Office. A flustered official rushed over to impart in a raised voice to the head of the unit next to me the news that Bill Clinton had just phoned the British Prime Minister, Tony Blair, about the International Criminal Court. It was an American spoiling game, to probe if, by going to the top at the last minute, the US President might subvert the efforts of the Foreign Office team in Rome to get agreement on a strong court. Such a court would potentially be able to prosecute for war crimes and crimes against humanity anyone from front-line troops to presidents. The USA did not want such a court and did not want to be isolated in opposition to it. Our host was not best pleased.

In the event the Rome Statute was signed on 17 July 1998 by 120 states. The ratification process extended over four years with the Court officially inaugurated in The Hague after the appointment of 18 judges in March 2003. In several ways this was a milestone in the process of global governance. It created a permanent body in which clearly defined crimes against humanity could be impartially prosecuted and punished, provided they took place on the territory of, or at the hands of perpetrators who were nationals of, ratifying states. The Security Council of the UN might refer cases to the court – thus underlining its character as an agency of the international community.

The establishment of such a court was potentially an enormous step forward. The codification and elaboration of international law since the Second World War had created a yardstick against which to measure the performance of states on human rights, but, in the absence of any body capable of trying and punishing violators, this remained a process of at best naming, and sometimes shaming. The weakness of this approach was illustrated by the level of non-compliance with the Convention against Torture.

The two International UN Covenants on Civil and Political Rights, and Economic, Social and Cultural Rights represented the highest ethical aspirations of the 'international community' in the twentieth century, a notable achievement of the United Nations. But they remained aspirations. The United Nations relied on a process of reporting and investigation. The primacy of national sovereignty blocked legal redress and punishment. Indeed the UN explicitly ruled out acting on complaints of human rights violations until the 1970s. Only in 1993, after the Vienna Conference, planned in the raised hopes after the end of the Cold War, was the appointment of a High Commissioner on Human Rights agreed by the General Assembly, though provided with a derisory budget. The post presided over a luxurious undergrowth of rapporteurs, reports, convenants and conventions. The Vienna Conference sadly revealed the continuing unwillingness of states to subject themselves to effective control over their human rights abuses.

It was only in the 1990s, and in the context of military victories, that realistic possibilities for establishing effective international tribunals arose. These were set up in the aftermath of conflicts involving 'ethnic cleansing' in the former Yugoslavia and genocide in Rwanda. Following 'regime change', they addressed the worst violations perpetrated by the ousted, the defeated and their leaders. But as a modest expression of a more global vision of justice, 'universal jurisdiction', they afforded the opportunity for impartial international courts to work with some degree of success, without the taint of implementing 'victors' justice', at least not to the same degree as in the Nuremberg and Tokyo trials after the Second World War.

The problem remained capturing and bringing key instigators, violators and witnesses to court. After much pressure on the new Serbian government its past President, Slobodan Milosovic, was dispatched to the Hague court, and others followed. Mrs Biljana Plavsic, the former President of Serbian Bosnia was sentenced in February 2003. Some important convictions were made in Arusha against prominent Rwandan *genocidaires*, such as the former Prime Minister, Jean Kambanda, but at enormous cost and with chronic administrative incompetence after years of preparatory investigations.

That international law could 'thicken' and coalesce through the creation of viable legal institutions during the 1990s was in large part a product of a climate in which states were tentatively reaching out towards a new international order and regional arrangements after the Cold War. Membership of the European Union was already obliging European states to cede elements of national sovereignty. The incorporation of the European Convention on Human Rights into the law of its member states was finessed in the face of chauvinist citizens rarely aware of its full implications. The action of a Belgian court in June 2001 in prosecuting and finding guilty two Rwandan Benedictine nuns for crimes committed in Rwanda during the genocide illustrated another way in which 'universal jurisdiction' might operate. The nature of the crime in a supra-national legal framework, not where it was committed, nor the nationality of the alleged perpetrator, was the key consideration. The prolonged house-arrest of General Pinochet, and subsequent decisions of the Law Lords in London, showed how breaches of international law, and the abuse of citizens of other countries by highly placed state perpetrators of human rights violations, were losing the immunity from prosecution that had formerly prevailed.

It was important that these positive changes were taking place in the implementation of international law since its legal framework was cracking in other respects. By the end of the 1990s, humanitarian intervention was threatening to become contingent on little more than the interests of a few powerful nation-states led by the USA. The two over-fly zones and the Kurdish enclave carved out of Iraq after the Gulf War, with the approval or, at least, acquiescence of the Security Council in Resolution 688, were only reconcilable with the UN Charter with difficulty. An unprecedented assault on the UN's founding doctrine of national sovereignty, they were cosmetically presented as safe havens – as if they might be an expansion of a humanitarian corridor. Iraq was effectively in part occupied throughout the 1990s.

Protection of the Kurds made humanitarian sense. Containing Al-Qa'ida terrorism was and is necessary. But the warehousing of Taliban and Al-Qa'ida suspects at Guantanamo Bay in Cuba by the US military reflected a different, and a more cavalier, disregard for international humanitarian law. Such precedents indicated that international law, like national security, risked becoming what Kofi Annan feared: whatever strong states declared it to be and could impose on weaker states.

The struggle for the International Criminal Court was therefore more than a skirmish in the battle for universal jurisdiction. It symbolised on a global scale an ethically rooted conception of international law. As the most powerful country in the world, the USA felt able to conduct its foreign – and national – policy on the basis of 'might is right'. If this meant voting at times alongside countries like China and a few pariah states, so be it. No international body was going to see the light of day with the moral and legal authority to try US soldiers. The USA was isolated and the Court brought into being, albeit facing many inherent problems. It was the first example, with perhaps the exception of the almost contemporaneous Land Mines Treaty, of how collaboration between state and civil society actors could enhance diplomatic power to great effect.

The initial work on the International Criminal Court had been undertaken by the International Law Commission of the United Nations. The NGO Coalition for an International Criminal Court (CICC) was formed in 1995. Its aim was to make inputs into an inter-governmental Preparatory Committee, which was charged with drafting the text forming the substance of a statute for the Court. The coalition was convened by two of its official observers, the legal adviser of Amnesty International, Christopher Hall, and the Executive Director of the World Federalist Movement, William Pace. Though it became a broad-based coalition with women's, peace, religious and other groups, its core consisted of the large international human rights organisations and their associated lawyers and academics. The latter were later reinforced by Latin American and other national lawyers' and human rights organisations. The looseness of the structure was compensated for by a like-minded steering group made up of Amnesty International, Human Rights Watch, the International Commission of Jurists, Lawyers Committee for Human Rights and the Federation International des Ligues de Droits de l'Homme.

The success of the coalition relied on two features. Firstly the level of legal expertise marshalled by the human rights organisations, the legal culture of the civil society actors, was shared with the governmental representatives, making for accessibility and relaxed advocacy. Informal and highly productive meetings took place between NGO legal representatives and relatively like-minded state representatives between Preparatory Committee sessions. Secondly the division of labour in the coalition was cannily co-ordinated by the World Federalist Movement. The latter stood outside any parochial conflicts amongst the human rights advocates – who might otherwise have clashed as competitors – or between them and other sectors. Regional caucuses lobbied their national governments, thematic working groups dealt with gender, children, peace, victims, justice and 'faith-inspired' issues, and twelve expert groups tracked key sections of the draft statute document.[14]

The coalition tellingly did not run an alternative conference during the 1998 inter-governmental Rome conference despite its comprising by then 800 member organisations. It had adequate access to the main conference. Not all members of the coalition were successful in their advocacy. The peace caucus, which was essentially an anti-nuclear lobby basing its position on the 1996 Advisory Opinion by the International Court of Justice on nuclear weapons, failed to get any prohibition of weapons of mass destruction into the draft. This was largely because their basic anti-nuclear position never stood a chance of getting the support of the nuclear states whose vote for the Statute was critical. The women's caucus did better, largely because of the findings of the Yugoslavia tribunal; systematic rape was officially acknowledged as a distinctive war crime. This highlighted the specific violations against women in war. In this context, there were skirmishes with religious groups around the meaning of 'forced pregnancy'. The final Rome Statute defined a variety of sexual crimes against women as crimes against humanity. A sophisticated advocacy programme and analysis of opportunities had allowed almost all of the women's goals to be attained.[15]

The overall success of the coalition at the conference stemmed from its highly professional control and dissemination of high quality information. The degree of success might be measured by the acceptance of the key contested provision: an independent prosecutor for the Court who could initiate investigations without going through the Security Council or member states. This was finally accepted against the wishes of the USA with the proviso that investigations had to have the permission of a pre-trial chamber of judges. This was an interesting outcome in that the CSOs held out for, and won, a position that moved beyond an international level of control to the – notionally – 'global', the independent prosecutor. However, five years later no one had been appointed. The advocacy goals of the CSOs, with the exception of those of the peace groups, broadly coincided with the interests of a significant multilateralist inter-state grouping.[16]

The negotiations surrounding the formation of the International Criminal Court illustrate constructive alliances between intergovernmental and INGO coalitions in the creation of a 'level playing field' organisation against entrenched US opposition. The relatively high level of independence of an international judiciary meant that everyone brought before the Court might expect equal treatment of their case irrespective of nationality. The same principle also applies to the disputes procedures of the World Trade Organisation, WTO. But here the dynamics of government–civil society interaction are somewhat different.

PATENT IMMORALITY

The price of multilateralism for the least developed countries is in practice to accept 'that the rules are written by – and usually for – the more developed countries'.[17] This is apparent when it comes to weapons of mass destruction as the ICC negotiations showed. Nonetheless the USA was unable to emasculate the ICC. Nor did it prove a deal-breaker that the US was defeated. Overwhelming US economic power exerted through the WTO, on the other hand, results in a different outcome.

In the Uruguay Round of the GATT/WTO, the USA got 95% of what it wanted and in subsequent meetings was unwilling to countenance substantive change to its agreements. This state of affairs resulted in the least developed countries adopting cautious strategies on Trade Related Aspects of Intellectual Property Rights (TRIPS) over the problem of pharmaceutical trade patenting. Their tactics were at variance with the strategies of the INGOs who were going for radical change in what they saw as a pernicious deal.[18]

The HIV/AIDS threat was overwhelming a number of African countries and the least developed countries saw pharmaceutical trade patenting in the context of this devastating scourge. The number of people living with HIV/AIDS worldwide rose from 37 million in 2001 to 42 million in 2002. Of the 3.1 million people who died of the disease in 2002, 77% of the deaths occurred in sub-Saharan Africa. Infection rates range from 40% of the population in Botswana downwards. Patenting was a matter of life and death.

One of these deaths has stuck in my mind, the young head of the Catholic Development Agency in Malawi, a gaunt and sallow man whom I met in the corridor of a small tin-roofed centre in Lilongwe where he was working in 2002. A well-educated lay leader, he was entrusted by his bishops with all the Catholic Church's development projects. His trousers seemed to hang off him, but I thought nothing of it. There is little fat on young men from Africa's rural areas. Two weeks later I asked after him and he had died of AIDS. It is people like him, the teachers and key government personnel, who are dying as well as the farmers, their wives and children. Grandparents are rearing large families of orphans. The economic impact will soon be devastating.

In the developing world only 4% of those infected with HIV get the cocktail of retroviral drugs that prolongs life. Half of these live in Brazil. The full market cost is $10,000 per patient per year but with generic, unbranded drugs it is possible to provide treatment for about $350 per person per year. Even this is far beyond the means of most of the least developed countries, as is the supervision of treatment that is required. Since prolongation of life is essential for the continuing viability of the economies of several sub-Saharan states with high HIV incidence, this is not merely a medical matter, nor simply a question of allocating a small health budget.

It was for this reason that TRIPS, patenting and public health, came onto the agenda of the inter-governmental WTO ministerial meeting at Doha in November 2001. Representatives of the developing nations had been under overwhelming US pressure to go beyond the current Uruguay TRIPS rules to accept what was dubbed TRIPS-plus. The US policy was evidently to secure the interests of the large pharmaceutical companies. The best the poorer countries could hope for was to obtain public clarification of unclear and ambiguous provisions in their favour. The US was exploiting these by insisting on interpretations in the companies' interests.[19]

The most important provision in the agreement was the possibility, left vague, of declaring a national emergency. Then, and only then, did it become permissible for governments to issue compulsory licences, licensing the manufacture of local generic drugs, which enabled, for example, the purchase of cheap generic retrovirals and drugs to reduce mother-to-child transmission. As if the eccentric views of President Thabo Mbeki that AIDS-related illnesses were not directly caused by the HIV virus were not enough, South Africa was targeted by the USA in 1999. One of the worst affected countries in southern Africa, it was threatened by the Clinton administration with sanctions, removal of special trade preferences, by way of a warning for 'non-compliance' with TRIPS-plus. With this stigma, loss of authorisation to borrow from the IMF and World Bank was also on the cards.

The TRIPS agreements contained within them enough flexibility for the poorest nations to find legal ways not to buy expensive brand names, or, at least, negotiate their price down with the pharmaceutical companies through threats of imposing compulsory licences. All they asked for was for these provisions to be applied 'without fear of litigation and sanctions', and for the existing TRIPS agreement to be enforced. This was a realistic position given the power and intransigence of the USA, and the problems they would confront with a continuation of its bullying. So the demand of affected governments was for TRIPS provisions to be nailed down. They were all for a level playing field. The INGO position, represented by organisations such as *Médecins sans Frontières* was different: to campaign for a roll-back of the TRIPS provisions in the interests of the poorest.[20]

At best, INGO pressure at the Doha WTO conference put the compliant position of the developing countries in a moderate light, not obviously anti-American. Moreover, vigorous INGO advocacy put pressure on the pharmaceutical companies and countered their lobbying of their governments. The US had already begun to back off on the question of retrovirals for sub-Saharan Africa, probably reacting to the political clout of black Americans and AIDS campaigners in the USA. Fears of biological attack after the October 2001 anthrax deaths in the USA raised the possibility of their also seeking to mass produce generic vaccines for inoculation under the 'national emergency' rubric. The Bayer company was obliged to slash its prices for CIPRO, an anti-anthrax vaccine, against the threat of a compulsory licence for North America, first mooted by Canada. This blew a hole in the US position leaving it open to a charge of double standards. A declaration finally emerged from Doha affirming the public health concerns of the developing countries and agreeing that, provided the WHO confirmed a country's declaration of a national emergency, as laid out in the Uruguay TRIPS agreement – not, as the Americans had wanted, on the say-so of the USA – exceptional measures would prevail. HIV/AIDS and other epidemic diseases were explicitly mentioned in the Declaration as grounds for such an emergency.[21]

Perhaps the greatest impact of this 2001 NGO campaign was on the pharmaceutical companies themselves, which, having gone to court in South Africa to protect their retroviral patents, faced extraordinarily negative publicity. In a world of brand and logo, INGOs' ability to puncture the fantasy worlds of the great logo companies, built up by vast advertising budgets, has become an Achilles heel. Publicising the companies as being engaged in a zero sum game of profits and dying people not only undermines the morale of their workforce but also hurts them more directly and financially. Ethical shareholders may want to sell. A lot of expensive image making and ethical preening goes down the pan. The more the customer buys the logo rather than the product, the more the vulnerability to unpleasant facts about the company's real operations. In April 2001 the pharmaceutical companies dropped their case in the South African courts and drastically reduced charges on some retrovirals.

Similar pressure has, of course, been put on companies such as Nike and Gap which are particularly susceptible to campaigns about the labour conditions of those who actually produce rather than market their sports goods and clothes. Shell, the butt of the environmental lobby, sets great store by the morale of its workforce and suffers if employees are called to task outside the workplace after Greenpeace stunts – not to mention the destruction of their carefully cultivated 'green image'. Nestle is dogged by the perseverance of health monitors of its milk powder marketing. Likewise the idea of 'conflict' or 'blood diamonds' troubles the emollient, romantic portrayal of De Beers in their product advertisements. This provides another cautionary story featuring the soft underbelly of corporate soft power.

DIAMONDS ARE FOR REBELS

Conflict Diamonds: Possibilities for the Identification and Certification and Control of Diamonds was published by a London-based INGO, Global Witness, in May 2000. It followed their report, *Rough Trade*, on the illegal Angolan trade commissioned by the UK Environmental Investigation Agency two years earlier. The report put De Beers and the governments of the USA, UK, Israel and Belgium, particularly the Diamond High Council in Antwerp, together with the UN, firmly in the dock. Each had contributed to the failure to block the flow of smuggled diamonds passing to African rebels and fuelling the Angolan civil war. Global Witness with two other Dutch INGOs accompanied their research with a campaign called 'Fatal Trans-actions' – revealing how the exploitation of natural resources funds wars. In a short time they projected onto the immaculate 'carat, colour, clarity and cut' of De Beers' product the real world of conflict and corruption.[22]

The spotlight was not welcome. The diamond campaign was

instructive in that it produced an extraordinarily fast response from De Beers and concerned governments. Firstly De Beers cut back on purchases from Angola and then agreed not to purchase from any rebel-held areas. Then governments launched the 'Kimberley Process', led by South Africa, which attempted to institute a national certification scheme as part of a tracing mechanism for import and export verification. But if tracking a BSE-infected cow back to source by a willing government is difficult, how much more difficult is creating a 'chain of warranties' tracking back a tiny diamond, by foot-dragging governments who rapidly lose interest once the heat is off? Global Witness's achievement is not untypical of other instances of INGO pressure on government; the initial public response is notable, and apparently promising, while later government performance is disappointing. The proof of the advocacy lies in the monitoring once companies and governments have regained their poise after the initial shock of INGO campaigning.

Cases such as these refute the idea that effective CSO action demands an attitude of perennial contestation with government and business. CSOs can raise the cost to business and government of doing nothing to unacceptable levels. But the attention span of the mass media is brief. Sustaining a high level of pressure may prove extremely demanding. CIIR championed the right of the East Timorese for self-determination for 25 years, whilst warding off suggestions that such advocacy was utopian, expensive and unrewarding. Whether it is campaigning or becoming operational in some form of service delivery, CSOs suffer from time, space and financial constraints. When their work is scaled up, or of long duration, they eventually need governments to step in if their goals are to be achieved. Successful monitoring and curbing of illegal and profitable activities require sustained state or inter-governmental intervention. This, as the aborted weapons inspection in Iraq illustrated, requires considerable political will. The nub of the problem for CSOs remains the translation of successful civil society action into institutionalised state intervention without loss of vision or effectiveness. And this requires a shared vision of how state and civil society can best promote democracy, peace and human rights together.

CIVIL SOCIETY AND INTERNATIONAL RELATIONS

The examination of these three examples tries to make a simple point: that in retrospect the 1990s may be seen as heralding the birth of 'global civil society' as something more than a vague idea. The peaceful resolution of that most internationalist of concerns, apartheid in South Africa, took place between 1990 and 1994. It was a success story involving the different layers of what, for once, might be called 'the international community' acting together to avoid violence and securing free and fair elections. The Church involvement was innovative. During 1993 and 1994, the Ecumenical Monitoring Programme of the Churches in South Africa (EMPSA) brought together Christians of many different nationalities, and many different Churches, to act as peacekeepers and monitors in the interstices where Commonwealth and UN observers were unable or unwilling to go. Churches operating locally, nationally and internationally had a head start in positioning themselves as global actors.

This experience provided a fascinating glimpse of what global civil society might look like in action in the future. As a bag-carrier for Kenneth Kaunda, I saw at first hand how effective an international 'Eminent Persons Group' could be in politically charged situations such as Kwazulu-Natal. But the key work was done by the scores of monitors who were there when the UN, Commonwealth, EU and the 'eminent persons' went back to their hotels. This experimental intervention to promote democracy was closely followed by more formal recruitment by the UN of groups of international monitors for peacekeeping and elections in Haiti.

Sadly these interventions proved to be the high point of co-ordinated internationalism. By the end of the decade, the Indonesian military and their local militia had systematically trashed East Timor leaving the UN and the monitors sent for the referendum on independence trapped in an unprotected compound in Dili. The final slaughter in East Timor had been long predicted, not least by the UN's own Intelligence personnel on the island. INGOs had lobbied to avoid it in vain. Earlier appeals for solid military back-up had been refused. Internationalist commitments to democracy and minority rights, no less than to humanitarian relief, more often than not need significant military support and, more important, the political will to provide and use it. A large number of individuals and European INGOs involved in the aid effort and solidarity actions during the Bosnian war of 1992–1995 also had to stand back and watch the UN humiliated as its forces presided over the massacre of 8,000 men in the 'safe haven' of Srebrenica and the systematic rape of women by Serb and Croat forces throughout the Balkans. What was becoming known as 'the responsibility to protect' was shaping up as one of the most contentious ideas in the arena of rights and responsibilities.[23]

The 1990s entente cordiale between state and civil society was, and remains, fragile. The fissure lines grew in the recent Gulf War. During the Rwandan refugee crisis after over a million people fled into the Congolese forests, OXFAM's head of emergencies accused the USA of falsifying aerial reconnaissance pictures to avoid acknowledging the magnitude of the problem. To do so would have resulted in pressure to send troops. INGOs had themselves been at each others' throats over the diversion of humanitarian relief in the Congo by the Rwandan *genocidaires*. In short we are still a long way from establishing models for humanitarian relief, peacekeeping, let alone environmental protection, democratisation and the promotion of human rights that involve close collaboration between agents of globalisation from above and from below.

Each instance, failure or success, has its own unique features. But where is the global learning organisation that learns and digests the lessons? In the exercise of the responsibility to protect, the complex interaction over time of networks of INGOs with multinational corporations and hierarchical inter-governmental bodies is evolving. But the direction is unclear. Suffice to say that the ethical impetus behind the movement towards, say, creating international protectorates such as that in East Timor prior to full independence, a universal jurisdiction for human rights abuses, or a global strategy to counteract global warming, will not abate. The question for global civil society is how and with whom.

The best way to sum up what is going on is that the slow gestation of a global civil society is opening up a range of new dilemmas and questions about how to safeguard the transcendent dignity of the human person in an emergent network society and its hinterland.

CSOs are exploring in action what might be meant by justice in the twenty-first century in the face of gross inequality, the shifting contours of international relations and the birth of an information economy. These are early days. The task is to find a usable ethics in the midst of these movements for justice, position them in a wider and more democratic context, and thus generate a politics fitting for an era of globalisation.

CHAPTER 8

MORAL SENTIMENTS IN THE TWENTY-FIRST CENTURY

This book unashamedly has been preoccupied with the role of civil society in the political economy of globalisation. Civil society resistance to the globalising economy, and the world it brings into being, has been a striking feature of the last decade. The growth of national and global civil society looks equally set to be a significant political expression of the new age, and an important new factor in international relations. Yet its potential is difficult to evaluate with any certainty in the midst of contemporary change. It may in the end prove a diversion from the difficult task of building pro-poor political parties. It is difficult to see, particularly in countries whose political cultures are hostile to an option for the poor, how civil society organisations can substitute for pro-poor, pro-ecology, parties able to take state power, or what is left of it in the future. In a sense, civil society in democratic states is at present substituting for the failures of other potentially more effective bearers of political purpose, and like candle light in the dark, shedding glimmers of the global common good.

That this should be so is because socialism and Christianity have failed to find adequate political forms to implement their parallel visions. Ethical concern for the common good drew people to socialist internationalism in the last century and – at least initially – motivated them. The Church's antipathy to, as it saw it, an anti-clerical creed based on class hatred, abated somewhat, at least temporarily, in the 1960s. A generation of Christians found in the themes of John XXIII's *Pacem in Terris* (Peace on Earth), the universal common good, human rights, the importance of the United Nations, an official blessing for reaching out to the secular world and participating in joint action. In Paul VI's *Populorum Progressio* (The Progress of Peoples) they found delineated the challenge of global injustice and poverty. In the World Council of Churches Programme to Combat Racism they saw courageous and costly political commitment. They wanted politics to become what it evidently was not, ethics as justice. I will own up to that. Nor am I ashamed of being part of a generation that tried creatively to make it so in a variety of ways, from Amnesty International to Christian Aid and CAFOD, to solidarity movements and democratic socialism.

But the last 40 years delivered a decisive verdict on socialism: human nature made it a utopian dream, latterly a rearguard action against Reagan/Thatcherism or, in its communist form, an existential horror. There is no easy ideological solution to the human ethical quest. Instead we inherit the messy and ambivalent world of global economics, civil society and – if we are lucky – democratic states, as the terrain on which to build the New Jerusalem.

A great deal of political energy has gone into rearguard action. Social democratic parties such as New Labour, with ingenious tactics for making redistribution palatable to middle England, the perseverance and patience of Lula's Brazil, the unexpected case of communist Kerala, for example, represent a spectrum of strategies. But a great deal of energy has also gone into 'values-led' civil society organisations – that do not have the same daunting task of persuading a majority of society, people with diverse values difficult to discern, to assent to their purposes. Civil society organisations (CSOs) are not, of course, led exclusively by values but by fallible individuals holding those values, with greater or lesser ability to hold onto them in adversity, and to get others to 'own' them within functional or dysfunctional structures. And, as discussed earlier, not all of these movements are benign.

Civil society organisations work best in democracies. And modern forms of democracy are the best political configurations that we have, at the moment, for arranging how states are governed with an ethical concern for justice. But prone to structural limitations, not least chronic short-termism related to electoral cycles, they are far from ideal. An enthusiasm for democracy and justice, as South Africa showed, is quickly tempered by the harsh winds of economic expedience linked to demand for high levels of mass consumption. CSOs may sometimes act as a counter to the power of consumer interests, and the partial judgement of those who do not care to think beyond immediate advantage and the short term. But it still represents a weak and fragmented opposition. The fact remains that in democracies the elected, or electable, political party continues to be the pre-eminent bearer of effective political purpose.

In responding to long-term dangers – not so long-term by most calculations – of ecological crisis, global warming and the squandering of the world's non-renewable resources, democracies have a tragic record. Is the modern democratic republic indeed, as John Dunn, Cambridge Professor of Political Science, suggests, 'a single extravagantly powerful mechanism for the inadvertent collective suicide of an entire species'?[1] Well, communist states poisoned large areas of the ex-Soviet Union and eastern Europe and proved even more damaging. But it is hard to dissent from the general proposition that we should see 'the victory of the very short term over the long term as the emblematic mode of human moral and spiritual defeat'.[2] It is the clear and present danger of this defeat that lends urgency to the quest for a shared ethics today.

So how are fundamental changes in our myopic political vision to be brought about? Structural sin has been, and is, a helpful concept in avoiding an unrealistic, individualist and voluntarist approach to political change. Structures need to be changed. We need a new enlarged UN Security Council, a new financial architecture that controls capital flows in the interests of the poor, and democratisation of international institutions, which currently suffer from a chronic democratic deficit. Politics as the art of the possible has to encompass large-scale innovative upheavals as well as small incremental ones within 'immovable' structures. But what comes after sinful structures are swept away or drastically reformed, and, it is hoped, their personnel changed for those with different political intentions?

The change from colonial to post-colonial world, it hardly needs saying – and V. S. Naipaul has said it trenchantly enough – was a necessary historical transition, not a glorious liberation. The lesson is that there is no such thing as a liberating and trustworthy state institution staffed by corrupt people, nor, come to that, 'values-led' organisations with staff uncommitted to the values. There is no escaping the truth that democratic political institutions and structures need virtuous people. This is as true of elected trades union officials as of voters in local and national elections. A just society can only be created and sustained by virtuous citizens. That this brings us to a far more intractable 'how' question does not make the proposition naïve or simplistic.

The frequent recurrence as pejorative terms of 'nanny state', 'directive', 'moralising', 'judgemental' or 'paternalistic', does not indicate wide social approbation for ethics or formative political action today. The pronouncement in 1997 by the then Foreign Secretary, Robin Cook, that Britain's foreign policy would have an 'ethical dimension' was widely treated with cynical derision. The question arises: when ethics may barely speak its name in the public domain where and how in the twenty-first century will moral formation occur?

Some occurs under the umbrella of government policy and recommended management practice. Institutions incorporating key functions of the state are perhaps the most forgotten loci of moral formation today. As part of their 'mission', they require certain values to be instantiated in daily institutional practice, and these values have to be transmitted effectively to most, though not necessarily everyone in them. The phrase used is tellingly that people have to 'own' the values. Much of this ethical negotiation is hidden by management-speak but all would agree that it is a core aspect of corporate and institutional life.

This kind of moral formation as a role of the state is obviously far from a universal phenomenon. For those knowing only kinship and ethnic relations, or forced to rely on them, state institutions merely provide a powerful arena for solidarities that generate a normative form of corruption. The idea of the *impartial* civil servant requires cumulative experience to become real and significant for professional conduct. It does not simply happen after citizens vote in democratic elections – as the Balkans illustrates. From those knowing only fear or hunger, and tyranny's assault on the ethical foundation of society, it would be romantic not to *expect* 'anti-social behaviour' – whether from state officials or ordinary citizens. The first thing some of the Iraqi people did when fear of the Baathist Party abated after the second Iraq war was to loot shops, hotels, hospitals, museums, offices and universities. But whatever the ambient cultural milieu, a clash of values has to be overcome – if only setting aside some expressions of individual liberty in favour of majority decisions – if an institution is to express effectively its fundamental ethical and political concern in action.

Moral formation is acknowledged, of course, as a role of religious organisations and schools. Churches are taken to be in the business of creating good Christians, communities formed around mosques, good Muslims, schools, good citizens. 'Citizenship' in Britain, newly introduced into schools, is taught patchily across the curriculum in the context of multiculturalism and human rights. What Churches and the democratic state recommend and encourage need not obviously clash. But the basic problems of the liberal state are thereby glossed over.[3] A good Muslim may not believe that the modern nation-state is the most desirable political configuration, and may find its legal system repugnant to faith. A good Christian may find conscientious reason for being a 'bad' citizen if assent to something contrary to conscience is demanded. Such clashing values and unquiet minorities are the Achilles heel of liberal democracy, with tolerance its only immediate answer.

So neither in schools, nor even in Churches, are people introduced to a holistic vision of what *politics* might be as an ethical commitment at the heart of citizenship and life. There is no clamour for more civic education. Islam for better or for worse has retained the vision. True, for Catholics there is the cumulative tradition of Catholic social teaching. The diligent may, and do, accumulate bits and pieces of precepts, rules, duties, rights and concepts of just and unjust international relations, assimilated individually, and acted on according to conscience. And a few may be motivated to undertake a lifetime's political engagement. What role the totality of this teaching might play in 'integral human development' as a political project is an open question.

In the lived culture of the Churches, for the most part, the message concerning the two principal terrains of political struggle in contemporary democracies, the political party and the mass media, is caution rather than prudence understood in its ethical sense. 'Politics' is that in which Church leaders should not dabble. The mass media is that which will distort the Church's teaching and statements. Understandable reactions. But this is a message that relegates leadership in the formation of political 'character', the quest for justice, to a marginal role in the life of the Churches, when it should be central.

The politics of the common good comes down, one way or another, to the bedrock of character. Why should democratic politics be the art of fooling electorates, spin and dissimulation? What kind of people are required in the twenty-first century to reverse a slow and relentless decline towards human catastrophe? Few advocate an educated fatalism. The question is how such people might be encouraged and enabled to develop the intentions, virtues and moral judgements that will avoid this fate.

As St Francis advised Christians going to live amongst Muslims: 'Preach the Gospel with all your heart, and, if necessary, use words.' Or if he didn't, he might well have. Ethical living takes place in communities in which virtues can be learnt by doing, and watching others doing. It is both about the formation of individual character and how society should be organised. There are communities and structures, in which individuals may learn virtues and communities, structures and social groupings, in which they cannot.

So setting structures against individual virtues in a chicken-and-egg paradox in a democracy is pernicious. Transparency, accountability, structures that control human weakness and encourage virtue, are an essential part of virtuous living. Multinational corporations with independently monitored codes of conduct are likely to instil virtuous behaviour and a recognition of values. Governments need audits and judicial review by independent bodies. Laws and rules reflect the formal ethical/political 'character' of individuals, society and state – as the apartheid regime illustrated in one way, Calvin's Geneva in another and New Labour's 2003 legislation on 'anti-social behaviour' in yet another. Though it must be said states do not behave like individuals and laws can sometimes be the fig leaves that hide disorder.

The future role and enduring importance of CSOs, their 'comparative advantage', lies here. Their positioning in relation to the family and state allows a unique freedom and potential for openness and dialogue, for learning what justice might be by doing it, and discovering what might be meant by an inclusive politics. They potentially have a pre-eminent role in the exploration of ethics. Their present position, what I can only call reluctantly an 'embedded marginality', suggests itself as a model for secular as well as Christian action across a wide ethical political spectrum. Indeed, amongst the CSOs, the major humanitarian organisations have already begun to adopt and promote ethical values that are shared across cultures by moving towards a simple ethical code of conduct. But to fulfil this role they have to look to their own democratic accountability and concern for truth.[4]

Projecting this ethical experience of civil society into the public domain in talk about human rights, 'issues' and campaigns has had some success, as the last chapter illustrated. But the limitations of this moral language, a compromised individualism and the fragmentation of political discourse, have also been discussed. Moreover, most people do not find themselves in communities in which they might readily discover what justice means in a complex world. Other people's practical wisdom on the matter cannot be sold them by the clever marketing of a compassion industry, or the snake-oil salesmen of Pentecostal evangelism. The demons are cast out, only to return, money given for the famine, only for famine to return. Something more and something less needs to be said and done. For the individualistic rich North, we need to be more sparing with rights talk and more precise in our talk about the universal common good; we have to 'thin' our human rights discourse and 'thicken' our discourse of the common good.

A basic anthropology on which a new politics of the common good might be built ought to start from beginnings no less basic than those chosen by Aquinas. Evidently a prior human right to self-preservation exists from which flow many of the hard-won rights of the UN Declaration, protocols and conventions. Human security might be a better phrase today than self-preservation. The primary responsibility of states is to ensure security – and define what they mean by it. It may be threatened in a variety of ways: for example by misrule, by suicide bombers, 'collateral damage' and the cavalier use of military might, by subsidised agriculture, mass marketing of fast food, nuclear proliferation or global warming. Much of the contemporary threat to human security stems from a simple defective understanding of the common good and a primitive concept of security.

Human beings have a second fundamental right that is little discussed and not directly alluded to in the UN Declaration: that is to meaning and moral formation. This might be expressed as a claim first on parents and family as a corresponding duty. Who is making the claim though? The answer 'the state on behalf of the child'

sounds sinister, redolent of re-education camps. It is more understandable as a statement about having and developing the faculty,
capability, capacity, to form moral judgements and to practise
virtues; a statement about human development and liberty. This is
an inalienable human right. Or, put in another way, 'an essential
requirement of the human person and the human community'.[5]

Amartya Sen's insight that human development is at heart about
the nurturing of human capabilities, and that such capabilities can
only grow in communities in freedom, provides a link between
Aquinas' thought and the best of development theory in the twenty-
first century.[6] A right to meaning and moral formation is grounded
self-evidently in natural law in that the capability for being virtuous
is fundamental and emblematic of all human agency. It is thus a
common human inheritance. Indeed the potential for ethical action is
the key to our – evolving – human nature. Nor is it unreasonable
to suggest that the flowering of human potential may imply some
direction and destiny that can barely be glimpsed in the short period
of human evolution to date.

So rights language may profitably translate, without loss, into talk
about capabilities and the language of human development and
global politics with the corresponding preconditions and obstacles to
their realisation, the need for both democracy and structural change.
The argument of this book is that the translation should be made
more often. The universal common good describes the horizon of the
only political project that can realise the completeness of human
identity and defeat the narrow identity politics of fundamentalism.
'It is not so much a matter of having exact rules about how precisely
we ought to behave', Sen writes, 'as of recognising the relevance of
our shared humanity in making the choices we face.'[7]

Integral human development, then, appears as nothing less than
the progressive realisation of a potential for ethical action,
demanding a democratic pro-poor politics that facilitates the nurturing of the other capabilities needed for human flourishing.
Poverty is its antithesis: the condition of being trapped in unjust
structures, prevented from developing these capabilities. But the pre-
condition for integral human development is building communities
with a culture of moral sentiments and language, the nurture of
virtue, and the winnowing of human desire.

It is in this context of human development that it makes sense to say people only have a *conditional* right to private property. This is a right conditional on the common good and the human security of *all*, particularly those in need. It is dependent on the practice of the virtue of justice – the poor of the least developed nations lack the most basic property right, most notably over their homes, and it is their due. De Soto argues that this is both a human rights violation that could be remedied by the state, and a fundamental obstacle to economic development in much of the world.[8] Virtues of temperance and fortitude amongst the citizens of affluent democratic nations are also a *sine qua non* for reducing their/our gross consumption of non-renewable resources, an urgent demand of the universal common good. In other words, people in the affluent world need to enjoy what they have more and find the courage to have less if we are to survive the century without catastrophe.

It follows from Aquinas' refusal to locate self-interest in opposition to the common good that there should be a natural priority in politics for preserving the 'goods' that can be shared by all, a theme to be found in the thought of the early Church and medieval canon lawyers. Indeed a major role of the state is the preservation and protection of these commons, the '*ta koina*', and of a politics that makes possible *koinonia*, sharing and participation. This ancient Christian principle of *koinonia* is found first in the Bible and then in the thinking of the fourth-century Church, Clement of Alexandria, St Basil the Great, St John Chrysostom and St Augustine. And this perspective leads directly to the today's concern for the 'global commons'.

Aquinas divided the world's resources into three categories: what is needed for survival, what people objectively require to perform their responsibilities – which might qualify any simplistic notion of equality – and the *superflua*, what he viewed as residual wealth. There is a duty in justice to dispose of superfluous wealth to the poor. A duty. Such distribution is not 'charity' because the poor have this as their due. The use of violence to retain such superfluous wealth is injustice, none other than the sin of robbery. So clinging to 'superfluous' wealth is not a minor matter. 'Since then to observe justice is necessary for salvation, to make restitution for what has been unjustly taken is likewise necessary.'[9] This was not just pious talk. Bishops in the fourth century acted on it or were harshly judged by their congregations on whether they distributed wealth according to Christian tradition and were 'lovers of the poor'.[10] So should we be.

In extreme situations all resources revert to being common resources for the poor. 'If the need be so urgent and evident', Aquinas wrote, 'that it is manifest that the immediate need must be relieved by whatever things occur . . . then someone may licitly take another's things to relieve his need whether openly or in secret. Nor does such action properly have the character of theft or robbery.'[11] His reasoning is that private property in such circumstances has ceased to fulfil its primary purpose of sustaining the human good. The *Summa*, given the rudimentary nature of state structures at the time, is unhelpful about the distributive powers of the state other than to reflect an emphasis on what is deserved in justice and what is merited. The focus is on justice as a personal responsibility. This responsibility in a democracy is fulfilled through citizenship, political engagement and the ballot box.

There is no escaping the conclusion that the uncontested right to private property and unrestrained financial wealth lies at the nub of our contemporary ethical dilemma. Finding such a state of affairs 'natural', necessary for market economics has to be checked, redefined in the direction of the original medieval limitation, as the right to own enough. The concept of 'too much', the superfluous, is surely comprehensible to societies dying of obesity as their neighbours, a plane ride away, die of hunger. It is hard to draw a precise *theoretical* line between the necessary and the superfluous but the scandalous facts of the global apartheid of poverty and affluence cannot be theorised away. They are glaringly obvious.

The consequences of incorporating this concept into contemporary politics should not be underestimated. To implement such a vision of just ownership in the setting of a modern economy would require crisis planning: a carefully co-ordinated project to counter an inevitable collapse of demand; incentives for investment in environmentally friendly technology and new research against diseases such as malaria, AIDS and SARS; stimulation of future demand not least throughout the continent of Africa, the creation of special intervention funds, are three obvious examples. It would need curbs, such as taxation, on the myriad financial transactions that generate vast hoards of unproductive wealth in symbolic forms as money, in order to pump prime faltering productive economies.[12] These are the hard facts of the existing situation. It would not be business as usual. And such extreme possibilities depend on a very different balance of power between states, the global market and civil society. They may impose themselves by the mid-century in a time of ecological crisis. It would be well to edge towards them before it is too late.

Finally, I hope this book has raised the question of the emerging shape of our world, and the shape of the moral life, which might begin to respond to it, in a way that encourages clarity about future action. But, at the risk of disappointing some, it would be a false ending to plunge into the realm of universal prescriptions and precise road maps. That is the perennial mistake of the World Bank. The model of ethical enquiry, recommended in chapter two, implies that we need to live in a particular way in order to find out what to do. That is if we wish to establish a genuinely transformative politics.[13]

Such an insistence on praxis is the core ethical message of liberation theology making the only 'road map' for the Christian community one that routes us via the Emmaus road. So to end up playing the casuist with the next set of global 'issues', writing a manual for the professional development advocate, or proposing yet another list of further recommendations, would be badly to miss the point. Prudential wisdom is given to those persevering on the journey called 'the option for the poor'. To believe that such discernment will indeed provide answers to our contemporary dilemma, thanks to the many different pilgrims on the journey, is the beginning of a sober hope.

Suffice to say, if future generations are to live in this way, it will require creating and nurturing communities, not least political parties, in which virtues can be learnt. So the real importance of civil society organisations for the twenty-first century is as vocational schools of prudential judgement and justice – from which a capacity for generating pro-poor politics will grow.

The moral language to engage with globalisation, to chart a viable political course on a new map of the world, will not come from the premature birth of a 'global ethic' – though heaven above knows it is urgent – but by the detailed practice of politics in a number of different structures, and by these practices being in genuine dialogue with each other. Global civil society is one such locus. The Church has the resources to be another, and, as a community, to be a meaningful embodiment and catalyst of a rational global politics. Whether it will do so depends on its openness to the future and its obedience to the Lord whom it worships.

NOTES

Introduction

1. The CIIR emerged from the wartime Sword of the Spirit in 1965 to specialise in advocacy in the sphere of international relations and development. It has programmes in eleven countries, placing development workers in projects in Latin America, Africa, Asia and the Middle East. Rooted in the Catholic tradition it works with peoples of all faiths and none. See M. Walsh, *From Sword to Ploughshare*, CIIR, London, 1980.

2. I use the term 'global apartheid' from time to time in the text to describe this. I am grateful to Titus Alexander for sending me his *Unravelling Global Apartheid: An overview of World Politics*, Polity Press, 1996 to illustrate his own use of the theme.

3. Structural power is 'the power to shape and determine the structure of the global political economy within which other states, their political institutions, their economic enterprises . . . have to operate' – see S. Strange *States and Markets*, Pinter Publishers, London, 1988, pp. 24–26.

4. Thomism describes the philosophical tradition that arose from the thought of Thomas Aquinas. The most notable twentieth-century exponent of the Thomist tradition in Catholic political thinking was Jacques Maritain who was offered a cardinal's hat as a layman by Pope Paul VI – but refused – see for example his two essays from the 1940s: J. Maritain, *Christianity and Democracy* and *The Rights of Man and Natural Law*, Ignatius Press, San Francisco, 1986.

5. S. Strange, *The Retreat of the State; the diffusion of power in the world economy*, Cambridge 1996 effectively rejects international relations as a discrete discipline for this reason.

6. Hans Kung is the President of the Foundation for a Global Ethic in Tubingen, Germany, see H. Kung, *A Global Ethic for Global Politics and Economics*, SCM, London, 1997.

7. See R. Plant, *Politics, Theology and History*, Cambridge, 2001, p. 141.

Chapter 1   **Political Education of an NGO-body**

1. R. Skidelsky, *John Maynard Keynes: Fighting for Britain 1937–1946*, Macmillan, 2000, pp. 403–458.

2. Quoted in R. Freeland, *The Truman Doctrine and the Origins of McCarthyism*, New York, 1991, p. 85.

3. This is the title of N. Sheehan's epic account of the Vietnam War, *A Bright Shining Lie*, Picador, London, 1990.

4. N. Mailer, *Harlot's Ghost*, Abacus, London, 1991.

5. See J. Slovo, 'Has Socialism Failed', South African Communist Party pamphlet, undated.

6. The quote comes from F. Fukuyama, 'The End of History', *The National Interest*, Summer 1989, pp. 3–4 and see F. Fukuyama, *The End of History and the Last Man*, Hamish Hamilton, New York, 1992.

7. See J. S. Nye, *The Paradox of American Power*, OUP, 2002, pp. 8–17. Strange, *States and Markets*, p. 26 emphasises control over production, security, knowledge and finance, which crisscross the economic, political and military categories.

8. S. Huntington, 'The Clash of Civilisations', *Foreign Affairs*, 72, 1994, pp. 22–49.

9. H. Gerth and C. Wright Mills, *From Max Weber: Essays in Sociology*, London, 1961, p. 47.

10. J. Gray, *False Dawn. The Delusions of Global Capitalism*, Granta, London, 1998. I cannot hope to deal with the delusions of post-modernism in the text so leave that to T. Eagleton, *The Illusions of Port-Modernism*, Basil Blackwell, Oxford, 1996, an excellent work of intellectual demolition which I wholeheartedly applaud.

11. M. Castells, *The Rise of the Network Society*, Blackwell, USA, 2000, p. 101.

Chapter 2   Dialogue Versus Flat-pack Ethics

1. E. Duffy, *The Stripping of the Altars: Traditional Religion in England 1400–1580*, Yale, 1992, p. 94.

2. B. Tierney, *The Idea of Natural Rights*, Scholars Press, Atlanta, Georgia, 1997 gives an outstanding account of the history.

3. M. Weber, *Economy and Society*, G. Roth and C. Wittick (eds.), New York, 1968, p. 902 – 'Politics as Leviathan is thus transformed into politics as symbol maker,' he reflects. And see M. Weber, *The Protestant Ethic and the Spirit of Capitalism*, S. Kahlberg (ed.), Blackwell, 2002, pp. xxv–xxvi.

4. 'We' is in inverted commas to indicate these problems of pluralism discussed in R. Plant, *Politics, Theology and History*, Cambridge, 2001. I am grateful to Raymond Plant for seminar discussions on liberalism at Cumberland Lodge, Windsor.

5. R. Williams, 'Beyond Liberalism', *Political Theology*, 3.1, 2001, p. 65 and see Archbishop of Canterbury's Dimbleby Lecture 2002 for further elaboration of these themes in terms of the 'market state'.

6. Williams, op. cit., p. 66.

7. Williams, op. cit., p. 65.

8. J. Rawls, *A Theory of Justice*, Clarendon Press, Oxford, 1972. Rawls only rectifies this in his later *The Law of Peoples* see P. Singer, *One World: the ethics of globalisation*, Yale University Press, 2002, p. 8.

9. H. McCabe, *Love, Law and Language*, Sheed and Ward, London, 1968, p. 60.

10. McCabe, op. cit., p. 61.

11. Williams, op. cit., p. 70.

12. McCabe, op. cit., p. 99.

13. Quoted from 'Economic Studies from Marx's notebooks' in *Karl Marx: Selected Writings in Sociology*, London, 1963, p. 129 by McCabe, op. cit., p. 60.

14. See for example M. Taylor, *Christian Ethics and World Development*, Mowbray, London, 1990 written while Director of Christian Aid.

15. A. MacIntyre, *After Virtue. A study in Moral Virtue*, Notre Dame, 1981.

16. See G. Gutierrez, *We drink from our own wells: the spiritual journey of a people*, Maryknoll/Orbis, 1984.

17. It may come as a surprise to some that Aquinas understood evil as either a deficiency or an excess of the good. Because of what he believed about the fundamental goodness of Creation, it followed that goodness could be asserted of all beings, so evil could only be a malign variation from the norm of the good – we would probably say 'mutation' of it. 'We have already seen that the good is whatever is desirable', Aquinas wrote, 'and since every nature desires its own being and perfection, it follows that the being and nature of any nature partakes of the character of goodness. Evil cannot, therefore, mean some being, or some form or nature . . . the term "evil" must mean some absence of good' (*Summa Theologiae* – henceforth ST – 1a, 48.1. The text is divided up into Prima Pars 1a, Prima Secundae 1a2ae, Secunda Secundae, 2a2ae and Tertia Pars, 3a).

18. J. Porter, *The Recovery of Virtue*, SPCK, 1990, p. 63.

19. N. Sagovsky, 'Thomas Aquinas on Justice', in J. Orme Mills ed., *Justice Peace and Dominicans*, Dublin, 2001, p. 33 and J. Finnis, *Aquinas*, Oxford, 1998, p. 45.

20. Finnis, op. cit., pp. 23–26, 80–87.

21. 'Habitus' is poorly translated as 'habit' because habits are usually bad ones. It means rather a stable and firm disposition to sustain a course of activity, as in habitual goodness.

22. See Amartya Sen, *Resources, Values and Development*, Harvard, 1984, pp. 307–325 and *Development as Freedom*, Oxford, 1999.

23. ST 1a, 95.3.

24. For this as for much of this section I have been greatly helped by Prof. Denys Turner and notes to his lectures for insights.

25. Porter, op. cit., p. 124.

26. 'Actus justitiae est reddere debitum' – the just act is that which renders what is due – ST 1a, 21.1.

27. Porter, op. cit., p. 160.

28. ST 2a2ae, 47.12–52.1 illustrates to what degree Aquinas saw prudence as pre-eminently the virtue of government.

29. Porter, op. cit., p. 127.

30. ST 2a2ae, 68.3.

31. ST 1a2ae, 100.2 quoted in Finnis, op. cit., p. 224.

32. ST 1a2ae, 96.3 quoted in Finnis, op. cit., p. 225.

33. Porter, op. cit., p. 67.

34. ST 1a, 96.4; ST 1a2ae, 1.2; ST 2a2ae, 57.1 from introduction by Marcus Lefebure to ST 2a2ae, 63–79.

35. Plato, *The Republic*, Penguin Classics, 1987, p. 448 associates five forms of character each with a particular form of state. 'Vice-versa' is intended to raise the question what character or characters – in the Platonic sense – might be associated with the network or market state.

36. See E. F. Schumacher, *Small is Beautiful*, Abacus, London, 1973, which is greatly influenced by Buddhism. A Catholic non-instrumental, non-reductionist and comprehensive development approach that factors in religion goes back at least to L. J. Lebret and R. Moreux, *Manifeste d'Economie et Humanisme*, Marseille, 1942, with Denis Goulet as its leading contemporary

exponent, see D. Goulet 'Development Experts: The One-Eyed Giants', *World Development*, Vol. 8, 1980, pp. 481–489.

Chapter 3 The Dark Underside of Globalisation

1. This is now changing, see Christian Aid's *Fuelling poverty: Oil, War and Corruption*, 2003; and the Publish What You Pay (PWYP) campaign backed by George Soros and involving a number of NGOs.

2. There is nothing new about corruption itself in bureaucracies. Amartya Sen gives examples from the *Arthashastra* of forty ways in which corrupt officials in the fourth century BC could be tempted to be corrupt, see Sen, *Development as Freedom*, pp. 275–276. For relationships to liberalisation see 'Liberalisation and the New Corruption', *IDS Bulletin*, Vol. 27, 2, April 1996.

3. Quoted in Amnesty International Report *Democratic Republic of Congo: Making a Killing: The Diamond Trade in Government-Controlled DRC*, 22 October 2002.

4. M. Castells, *End of the Millennium*, Blackwell, Oxford, 1998, p. 354.

5. Amnesty International Press Releases on Espirito Santo, Brazil, of 5, 9, 25 and 26 July 2002.

6. *Global Corruption Report*, 139, pp. 140–141.

7. op. cit., pp. 11, 47.

8. J. Carlin, 'The Zimbawbe Connection', *The Independent Review*, 28 November 2002, pp. 4–5; Amnesty Report on DRC, 22 October 2002.

9. 'Coca, Cocaine and the War on Drugs', CIIR *Comment*, 1993, pp. 2–13; Castells, *End of the Millennium*, pp. 190–196.

10. op. cit., pp. 170–175.

11. G. Barclay and C. Tavares, *International Comparisons of Criminal Justice Statistics*, Home Office, UK.

12. Bureau of Justice Statistics, Justice Department USA, 2003 and F. Butterfield, 'Prison Rates Among Blacks Reach a Peak in US', *The New York Times*, 7 April 2003. Castells concludes 'building more prisons to address crime is like building more graveyards to address a fatal disease.' op. cit., p. 149.

13. Associated Press, 10 September 2002.

14. Castells, op. cit., pp. 172, 177.

15. J. Doezema, 'Loose Women or Host Women: The Re-emergence of the Myth of White Slavery in Contemporary Discourses on Trafficking in Women', *Gender Issues*, Vol. 18:1, Winter 2000, pp. 38–64.

16. See J. Seabrook, *Travels in the Skin Trade; tourism and the sex industry*, Pluto Press, 2002 and Anti-Slavery International Report, *Whose Interests Served? A review of the obstacles to prosecution and measures to protect victims, especially those who act as witnesses, in the context of trafficking in persons*, June 2002.

17. Anti-Slavery International Report, *Whose Interests Served?*, and 'In the Belly of the Beast: Sex Trade, Prostitution and Globalisation' in *In the Belly of the Beast*, pp. 21–45.

Chapter 4 The Global Political Economy

1. Quoted in E. Rothschild, 'Globalisation and the Return of History', *Foreign Policy*, Summer 1999, p. 110.

2. A. G. Hopkins, *Globalisation in World History*, Pimlico, 2002, pp. 7–13.

3. P. Hirst and G. Thompson, *Globalisation in Question*, Polity Press, 1999, pp. 20–26.

4. J. M. Keynes, *The Economic Consequences of the Peace*, (1919), Penguin, London, 1988, p. 11.

5. N. Ferguson, *The Cash Nexus: Money and Power in the Modern World 1700–2000*, Penguin, 2001, p. 297 and *Globalisation in Question*, p. 22.

6. op. cit., p. 22.

7. J. S. Nye, *The Paradox of American Power*, OUP, Oxford, 2002, pp. 8–12.

8. R. Skidelsky, *John Maynard Keynes: Fighting for Britain 1937–1946*, Macmillan, 2000, pp. 337–372.

9. R. Wade, 'International Institutions and the US Role in the Long Asian Crisis of 1990–2000', paper presented at Tenth Anniversary Conference of the Development Studies Institute, LSE, September 2000.

10. R. Wade, 'From "miracle" to "cronyism": explaining the Great Asian Slump', *Cambridge Journal of Economics*, 22.3, November 1998, pp. 693–706; S. Griffith-Jones, J. Cailloux and S. Pfaffenzeller, 'The East Asian Financial Crisis', IDS Discussion Paper No. 367, September 1998; D. Woodward, 'Contagion and Cure: tackling the crisis in global finance', CIIR, *Comment*, 1999.

11. G. Soros, *On Globalisation*, Public Affairs, Oxford 2002, p. 117.

12. D. Held and A. McGrew, *Globalisation/Anti-Globalisation*, Polity Press, 2002, pp. 49–50.

13. Hirst and Thompson, *Globalisation in Question*, pp. 79–89.

14. S. King, 'Globalisation puts Fed's actions at centre stage', *The Independent*, 5 November 2001.

15. D. Coyle, 'It's time to review arms industry's £4bn subsidy', *The Independent*, 4 July 2001.

16. R. Brenner, 'Towards the Precipice', *London Review of Books*, 6 February 2003, pp. 18–23.

17. N. Boyle, *Who are we now?*, Notre Dame Press, Indiana, 1998, pp. 116–119, 315–317 discusses the advent of 'global proletarians'.

18. R. Kagan, 'The Power Divide', *Prospect*, August 2002, pp. 20–27 and *Of Paradise and Power: America and Europe in the New World Order*, Knopf, 2002. For an opposing thesis that capital expansion indicates an end of US hegemony, and the beginning of a 'hegemonic crisis', see G. Arrighi and B. J. Silver, *Chaos and Governance in the Modern System*, University of Minnesota Press, 1999.

19. K. Watkins, *Fixing the Rules: North-South Issues in International Trade and the GATT Uruguay Round*, CIIR, London, 1992; K. C. Shadlen, 'Patents, Public Health and the WTO: Developing Countries and the Strengthening of International Governance' Crisis States Programme Paper, DESTIN, LSE, 2002, p. 3.

20. 'Los campesinos de Mexico exigen cambios en el tratado con EE UU', *El Pais*, 1 February 2003.

21. D. Zerah, 'Bono, le Farm Bill et le coton africain', *Le Monde*, 22 June 2002.

22. Soros, *On Globalisation*, p. 33; *The Independent*, 2 June 2003 and see D. Green and M. Griffith, 'Dumping on the Poor', CAFOD/Christian Aid, September 2002.

23. J. Stiglitz, *Globalisation and Its Discontents*, Allen Lane/Penguin, London 2002, p. 176.

24. M. Larouche and S. Marti, 'Un besoin d'ancrage à la mondialisation', *Le Monde*, 26 June 2001.
25. CIIR Internal Briefing Paper on the WTO and Soros, *On Globalisation*, pp. 32–33.
26. Soros, op. cit., p. 33; F. Jawara and A. Kwa, *Behind the Scenes at the WTO: the Real World of International Trade Negotiations*, Zed Press, London, 2003.
27. Stiglitz, op. cit., p. 92.
28. op. cit., p. 13.
29. B. Fine, 'Neither the Washington Nor the Post-Washington Consensus: an Introduction', SOAS Seminar Paper, October 1998.
30. F. Stewart, 'Income Distribution and Development', UNCTAD X, 2/00,10 quoted in D. Green and C. Melamed, *A Human Development Approach to Globalisation*, CAFOD/Christian Aid, June 2000, p. 10.
31. Stiglitz, op. cit., p. 193.
32. J. Stiglitz, 'More Instruments and Broader Goals: Moving Towards the Post-Washington Consensus', WIDER Lecture, Helsinki, January 1998, p. 25.
33. Fine, 'Neither the Washington nor the Post-Washington Consensus', October 1998.
34. J. D. Wolfensohn, 'A Proposal for a Comprehensive Development Framework', World Bank paper, 21 January 1999 sets the scene.

Chapter 5   Changing Spaces

1. Castells, *The Rise of the Network Society*, p. 266.
2. op. cit., p. 100.
3. Castells, *End of Millennium*, p. 340.
4. See S. Strange, *The Retreat of the State*, Cambridge, 1996; P. Bobbitt, *The Shield of Achilles: War, Peace and the Course of History*, Allen Lane, 2002, pp. 667–797.
5. R. Williams, Dimbleby Lecture, 2002.
6. Castells, *End of Millennium*, p. 348; Address of Holy Father, *Globalisation. Ethical and Institutional Concerns. Acta*, Pontifical Academy of Social Sciences, Vatican City, April 2001, p. 29; J. S. Nye, *The Paradox of American Power*, OUP, 2002, pp. 69–74.
7. N. Klein, *No Logo*, HarperCollins, 2000; E. Schlosser, *Fast Food Nation*, Penguin, London, 2002, for food industry.
8. Castells, *The Rise of the Network Society*, p. 403.
9. op. cit., pp. 442–46.
10. The point is well made in a review of Castells' work by J. Crabtree, 'The Cult of Castells', *Prospect*, February 2002, pp. 50–54.
11. See also D. Held and A. McGrew, *Globalisation/Anti-Globalisation*, Polity Press, 2002, p. 33.
12. C. Crook, 'Globalisation and Ethics', St Paul's Seminar, 30 January 2003. Clive Crook is deputy editor of *The Economist*; C. Leadbeater, 'Globalisation: now the good news', *New Statesman*, 1 July 2002, pp. 29–31.
13. *The Paradox of Prosperity*, A Report for the Salvation Army, The Henley Centre, 1999, quoted in 'Prosperity and Poverty in the Context of Globalisation: Poverty in the UK', paper given by Hilary Russell to CCBI seminar on Prosperity in the UK, September 2002. 'Redistributing benefits or services away from the very poorest to those just below the poverty line actually deepens

the deprivation of the worst off,' she claims, supporting Lars Osberg's conclusion that poverty 'intensity' should be the key measurement of poverty, see 'Trends in Poverty: the UK in international perspective', Institute for Social and Economic Research Working Paper 10, 2002.

14. See P. Townsend and D. Gordon, *World Poverty*, Policy Press, Bristol, 2002; B. M. Friedman, 'Globalisation: Stiglitz's Case', *New York Review of Books*, 15 August 2002 and letter 'What is Poverty', 21 November 2002.

15. Castells, *The Rise of the Network Society*, p. 298.

16. op. cit., p. 410.

17. J. Madeley, *Hungry for Trade: How the Poor Pay for Free Trade*, Zed Press, 2001 gives the annual coffee trade as worth $8 billion, employing 25 million people in 80 different countries, 70% of them small farmers.

18. Quoted in P. Dicken, *Global Shift: Transforming the World Economy*, Paul Chapman, London, 1998, p. 465.

19. *Karl Marx and Frederick Engels Selected Works*, Moscow Languages Publishing House, Moscow, 1962, p. 36.

Chapter 6 **Resistance Movements**

1. Pope John Paul II deals with personal responsibility for structures of injustice in *Laborem Exercens* in 1981 and discusses 'structures of sin' in *Sollicitudo Rei Socialis* in 1987. For an excellent, succinct survey of key themes in Catholic social teaching see D. Dorr, *Option for the Poor*, Gill & Macmillan, 1983.

2. B. S. Turner, *Weber and Islam*, Routledge & Kegan Paul, London, 1974, pp. 7–21; Kahlberg, *The Protestant Ethic*, pp. I–XXVIII.

3. This is one of the conclusions that may be drawn from M. Castells, *The Power of Identity*, Blackwell, Oxford, 1998.

4. Klein, *No Logo*, pp. 50–61.

5. S. Huntington, 'The Clash of Civilisations?' *Foreign Affairs*, 72, 1994, pp. 22–49.

6. Though Iran's progressives strive to overcome differences in key areas such as human rights see *Human Rights and Dialogue of Civilisations*, collected papers of an international conference of this title, published by Mofid University Publications Institute, Qom, Iran, 2001.

7. For statistics on civil society see M. Glasius, M. Kaldor and H. Anheier, *Global Civil Society*, Oxford University Press, 2001, 2002, 2003 editions.

8. Klein, *No Logo*, pp. 365–396.

9. See for example the complex picture that emerges from 'Liberalisation and Poverty', an OXFAM-IDS Project Report, August 1999, on Zambia and Zimbabwe.

10. J. Madeley, *Hungry for Trade: How the Poor Pay for Free Trade*, Zed Press, 2000, p. 64.

11. *El Pais*, 1 February 2003; Madeley, *Hungry for Trade*, pp. 75–80.

12. Total Overseas Development Assistance spent on emergency aid rose in the decade 1988–1998 from $1.6 billion to $4.5 billion.

13. T. Sewell, *The World Grain Trade*, Woodhead-Faulkner, New York, 1992 gives a comprehensive overview.

14. See D. Green and M. Griffith, 'Globalisation and its Discontents', *International Affairs*, 78, 2002, pp. 49–68.

15. Castells, *End of the Millennium*, pp. 246, 258, 265; D. Woodward, 'Time to

Change the Prescription: A Policy Response to the Asian Financial Crisis', CIIR, *Briefing*, 1999.

16. Government was showing more concern with the speed and sequencing of liberalisation measures so much NGO concern was now focusing on the lack of regulation of private companies in the international arena, see BOND (UK NGO-Coalition), *The Network*, February 2001.

17. J. Madeley, 'No End to Shackles', *The Observer*, 21 January 2001.

18. Castells, *The Power of Identity*, pp. 31, 65–66.

19. D. F. Eickelman and J. Piscatori, *Muslim Politics*, Princeton 1996, pp. 48–51.

20. *The Independent*, 2 November 2002.

21. K. Maxwell, 'Brazil: Lula's Prospects', *New York Review of Books*, 5 December 2002, pp. 27–32.

22. E. Gellner, *Conditions of Liberty*, Penguin, London, 1994, pp. 50–52.

23. P. Freston, *Evangelicals and Politics in Asia, Africa and Latin America*, Cambridge, 2001; C. Smith and J. Prokopy (eds.), *Latin American Religion in Motion*, Routledge, 1999.

24. P. B. Clarke and I. Linden, *Islam in Modern Nigeria*, Kaiser Grunewald, Mainz/Munchen, 1984.

25. P. Mandaville, *Transnational Muslim Politics: Re-imagining the Umma*, Routledge, 2001, pp. 79, 134, 142, 158–164; J. L. Esposito (ed.), *The Oxford History of Islam*, OUP, 1999, pp. 601–691.

26. Clarke and Linden, op. cit., pp. 75–94.

27. I am indebted to Baqer Talebi, Seyed Amir Akrami, Sadegh Zibakalam and many others in Tehran and Qom for their insights into contemporary Iran during visits for inter-religious dialogue.

28. For example see the remarkable F. Esack's, *Qur'an Liberation and Pluralism. An Islamic Perspective of interreligious solidarity against oppression*, OneWorld, Oxford, 1997 and A. Ibrahim, 'The Ummah and Tomorrow's World', *Futures*, Vol. 26, 1999, pp. 302–310; J. L. Esposito (ed.), *Voices of Resurgent Islam*, Oxford, 1983.

29. There is a great deal of difference between the positions and contexts of each. For the sophisticated position of Al-Turabi see Y. F. Hasan, 'The Role of Religion in the North-South Conflict, with special reference to Islam' in Y. F. Hasan and R. Gray, *Religion and Conflict in Sudan*, Pauline Publications, Nairobi, 2002, pp. 39–41; for the context of Al-Madani's thought see H. Roberts, 'North African Islamism in the blinding light of 9–11', Crisis States Paper, DESTIN, LSE, March 2003 and *The Battlefield: Algeria, 1988–2002, Studies in a Broken Polity*, Verso, 2003.

30. Sayyid Qutb in Egypt and Mawlana al-Mawdudi in Pakistan are the intellectual origins of much of this movement, see J. Esposito, *Unholy War: Terror in the Name of Islam*, OUP, 2002, pp. 51–61.

31. J. Kelsay, 'War, Peace, and the Imperative of Justice in Islamic Perspective', undated paper, (2002) Florida State University.

32. ibid.

Chapter 7   **Global Civil Society**

1. E. Gellner, *Conditions of Liberty,* Penguin, London, 1994, p. 13.
2. Adam Ferguson, *An Essay on the History of Civil Society,* (1777), Farnborough, 1969.
3. A. de Tocqueville, *Democracy in America,* New York, 1848, Vol. II, Part II, Chapter Five deals with 'associations'.
4. Glasius, Kaldor and Anheier, *Global Civil Society,* 2002, p. 194.
5. E. Childers, *Challenges to the United Nations,* CIIR/St Martin's Press, 1994, p. 3.
6. Held and McGrew, *Globalisation/Anti-globalisation,* p. 18.
7. See P. Bobbitt, *The Shield of Achilles: War, Peace and the Course of History,* Allen Lane, 2002 for a wider picture.
8. Speech to UN General Assembly, 20 September 1999 quoted in P. Singer, *One World: the ethics of globalisation,* Yale, 2002, p. 126.
9. C. Archer and D. Hay-Edie, *Freedom from Fear. Freedom from Want. Human Security as a Path to Peace,* International Peace Bureau, Geneva, 2003 for example has extensive references to the key role of the UN. I am grateful to Bruce Kent for discussions on this and to Colin Archer for sending me a draft copy of the above.
10. Immanuel Kant, *Idea for a Universal History with a Cosmopolitan Intent,* 1784, 'The greatest problem for the human species, whose solution nature compels it to seek, is to achieve a universal civil society administered in accordance with the right ... There must be a society in which one will find the highest possible degree of freedom under external laws combined with irresistible power i.e. a perfectly just civil constitution.'
11. See J. Macrae and N. Leader, 'Apples, Pears and Porridge: The Origins and impact of the search for "coherence" between humanitarian and political responses to chronic emergencies', *Crisis States Working Paper,* DESTIN, LSE, 2003 for an excellent analysis of the origins of the problem.
12. See for example N. Chandhoke, 'The Limits of Civil Society' in *Global Civil Society 2002,* pp. 35–53 for a strong critique of this kind.
13. M. Moore and J. Putzel, 'Thinking Strategically about Politics and Poverty', *IDS Working Paper,* October 1999, p. 6.
14. The detailed material on advocacy at the ICC is drawn from the compelling analysis of M. Glasius, 'Expertise in the Cause of Justice: Global Civil Society Influence on the Statute for an International Criminal Court', *Global Civil Society 2002,* pp. 137–165.
15. ibid.
16. ibid.
17. This and subsequent detailed analysis of the negotiation is taken from K. C. Shadlen, 'Patents, Public Health and the WTO: Developing Countries and the Strengthening of International Governance', *Crisis States Working Paper,* DESTIN, LSE, 2002.
18. See for example *Patent Injustice: How World Trade Rules Threaten the Health of the Poor,* OXFAM, February 2001.
19. Shadlen, 'Patents', op. cit.
20. ibid.
21. P. Singer, *One World: the ethics of globalisation,* pp. 72–74.
22. This and subsequent detailed analysis of the diamond trade is taken from

N. Shaxton, 'Transparency in the International Diamond Trade', in *Global Corruption Report*, Transparency International 2001, pp. 214–222.

23. The term arose from the report of the International Commission on Intervention and State Sovereignty chaired by Gareth Evans and Mohamed Sahnoun, entitled 'The Responsibility to Protect'.

Chapter 8   Moral Sentiments in the Twenty-first Century

1. J. Dunn, *The Cunning of Unreason. Making Sense of Politics*, HarperCollins, 2000, p. 226.
2. op. cit., p. 200.
3. See R. Plant, 'Liberal Government, Civil Society and Faith Communities', *Political Theology*, May 2003, pp. 206–218 and, for citizenship in schools, A. Osler et. al. (eds.), *Citizenship and Democracy in Schools*, Trentham Books, 2000.
4. *Code of Conduct for the International Red Cross and Red Crescent Movement and Non-Governmental Organisations (NGOs) in Disaster Relief*, booklet printed by International Red Cross, Geneva; for the prerequisites for this role see J. Clark, *Democratising Development: The Role of Voluntary Organisations*, Earthscan, London, 1991, pp. 74–80 and *Worlds Apart: Civil Society and the battle for Ethical Globalisation*, Kumarian Press, Bloomfield, USA, 2003.
5. Address of Holy Father in *Globalisation. Ethical and Institutional Concerns*, pp. 28–29.
6. The theme of capability as a yardstick for development was introduced by Amartya Sen in his 1979 Tanner lecture 'Equality of What?'; see S. McMurrin (ed.), *The Tanner Lectures on Human Values*, Salt Lake City 1980.
7. A. Sen, *Development as Freedom*, Oxford, 1999, p. 283.
8. H. de Soto, *The Mystery of Capital. Why capitalism triumphs in the West and fails everywhere else*, Bantam Books, London, 2000.
9. ST 2a2ae, 62.2.
10. See P. Brown, *Poverty and Leadership in the Late Roman Empire*, University Press of New England, Hanover and London, 2002.
11. ST 2a2ae, 66.7.
12. For example to create a climate for Special Drawing Rights to be made available to the least developed nations, see Soros, *Globalisation*, pp. 71–79; and for massive intervention to block currency speculation, see Woodward, *Contagion and Cure*, pp. 33–35 and 'Time to Change the Prescription', CIIR, *Briefing*, 1999.
13. 'Transformational development' is now a major theme in some evangelical mission Christianity, see *Transformation*, April 2003, and the work of the Institute for Development research at the Oxford Centre for Mission Research. I am grateful to Prof. Deryke Belshaw for sending me proofs. What I mean by a transformative politics for development is more extensively outlined in M. Moore and J. Putzel, 'Thinking Strategically about Politics and Poverty', *IDS Working Paper*, October 1999.